BECOMING A
PRACTICAL
MYSTIC

For Kathy —
My mystical
Sister!
I love you —

BECOMING A PRACTICAL MYSTIC

CREATING PURPOSE FOR OUR SPIRITUAL FUTURE

JACQUELYN SMALL

A publication supported by
THE KERN FOUNDATION

Quest Books
Theosophical Publishing House

Wheaton, Illinois ♦ Chennai (Madras), India

The Theosophical Publishing House
P.O. Box 270
Wheaton, IL 60189-0270

A publication of the Theosophical Publishing House,
a department of the Theosophical Society in America

Library of Congress Cataloging-in-Publication Data

Small, Jacquelyn.
        Becoming a practical mystic: creating purpose for our
        spiritual future / Jacquelyn Small. — 1st Quest ed.
             p.   cm.
        Includes text of the author's previously published
        works: Becoming a practical mystic, Living your
        bigger story, and some new material.
        ISBN 0-8356-0770-4
        1. Spiritual life.   2. Mysticism.   I. Small,
        Jacquelyn. Living your bigger story.   II. Title.
        BL624.S5936   1998
        291.4'4—dc21   98-20484

        4   3   2   1   *   98   99   00   01   02   03

Printed in the United States of America

CONTENTS

INTRODUCTION:
BECOMING A PRACTICAL MYSTIC

*We must go where there is quality. We must under-
stand with the heart and create harmony wherever
we go. This is the Royal Road that leads us to the
merging of love, wisdom, and active intelligence. This
is the work of the mystic with a practical point of view.*

A few years ago when I was undergoing a major
crisis, I called a friend one evening for support.
I remember the most helpful thing she said to
me was, "Jacquie, I know this is a really terrible time
for you. But don't forget the bigger picture. Remember
what you're really here for—this crisis may just be part
of your clearing so you can better serve."

Upon hearing this reminder, my miserable feelings of the moment started to fall into perspective, and
I began to settle down. I knew I could cry out for help
from my inner guides and teachers, or even directly to
the Divine Power. I had already learned from my experience that when I cry out, there is always a response—
though sometimes the form it takes is quite a surprise.
This is no religious platitude; the power of invocation

and response follows a universal law.

In times of stress or need, divine guidance is just awaiting our call. This is a fact built right into the human psyche, a part of the divine plan. But because we live in a reality where there's free will, our plea must be heard before a Higher Order will tamper with our lives; we must give our permission.

When you decide to get fully behind your highest spiritual goals and aspirations, dedicating your life to service for the whole, the cosmic law of service becomes your guiding force. And once this happens, all else in your personal life gradually begins to fall into place. Everything in your life will take on new meaning, and you'll no longer feel that you're being tossed around by fate from one unrelated event to another.

This spiritual law was well known to our ancestors, who took their mystical perception for granted. But sadly, the great powers inherent in every human soul are no longer familiar to us.

This little book is a reminder that when we let our highest spiritual purpose and divine intention become the organizing principle behind our activities, we discover we're all practical mystics and miracle workers. Through the great power of invocation, we align with our greatest potential and become conscious participators in the divine plan for humanity—right here in our ordinary world.

I was taught this principle from the inside out quite dramatically at a critical point when I was on the verge of taking my life—a personal story I will share with you to give you hope and help remind you of your own inherent powers as a human soul. Unfortunately, it usually takes a personal crisis to open us to a higher realm.

Many years ago I had been going through a painful marital breakup. A hopeless romantic, I was devastated by the death of this passionate relationship. Convinced that I'd never love again, and believing my life had been for nothing, I wandered the streets like one lost, wishing more than anything that I could just die. I couldn't work; I couldn't eat; I could hardly even breathe.

I went home in despair and scribbled in my journal a desperate plea that welled up from my gut. (Perhaps you can relate to this feeling.) I demanded that a Higher Power lift me out of this awful mess I was forced to call my life! Little did I know that I was utilizing the ancient spiritual power of invocation. I didn't even know what the word meant. Stronger than falling on your knees in passive prayer, to invoke is to petition assertively the God of your understanding. You do this in the knowledge that you are a cocreator and have your part to do in any divine intervention. Here was my plea:

> I'm sick to death of this melodramatic life, moving from disaster to disaster. It's all making me sick! I demand to be lifted out of this mess I'm making of my life! I seek with all my might to be placed in the midst of my true purpose, so I will never again miss the point of this meager existence! I demand your

assistance this minute! I'm willing to do whatever it takes to connect with you right now.

Then I fell on my bed, brokenhearted. I thought if I got still enough and just quit breathing, maybe the Divine Power would be gentle and take me away. But instead, something awesome happened: A commanding voice boomed in my head, startling me greatly. I remember sitting straight up, saying to myself, "Okay, Jacquie Sue. Now, you've really lost it; you're having an auditory hallucination!"

The powerful voice ordered me to go into my library, find a classic esoteric text I'd owned for years but never read, and start reading on page 146! The instructions were that specific (and not in a tone one could easily ignore). So I found the book, turned to the page, and here is what it said (I paraphrase):

You are one who has the ability to voice truth through the written word. You know how to clothe ancient wisdom in modern-day garb. You can write a book in the field of an oncoming major science and service, the new psychology, a synthesis. This should be your main subjective task for the next several years. You are not to withdraw from life to write this book. It will be wrought out in the crucible of your own energetic experience. And as you proceed, you will meet others along the way you are to work with and help train.

Something deep inside me resonated with these words. Though they had been written in the 1930s to someone else, I knew this message was for me. What jumped out was the hope that something besides my miserable personal life was going to preoccupy me for the next several years. This gave me a reason to live.

I accepted my fate and dedicated myself to the task. After many false starts—even completely giving up at one point—I was moved by the Energy living inside my head that had ordered me to read that message. It took hold and manifested a book—*Transformers: The Artists of Self-Creation*. The seed thoughts in *Transformers* came to me spontaneously, usually while driving my car. I learned to keep a notepad with me at all times to catch the words that flowed from deep inside. The message was light-years ahead of what my ordinary ego brain knew.

I read parts of this book today and am still amazed. *How did I know that?* is the question that always comes. I am trained as a social worker and had at the time rarely traveled outside of Texas. I'm from uneducated parents who had few resources and brought me up in the First Baptist Church in Corpus Christi, Texas—hardly a foundation for metaphysical scholarship! I am living proof that *anyone* can be inspired and come fully into their life's work! I realize now that as I invoked that desperate plea, I was entering a new stage. A future was calling while my past dissolved.

Many years passed after that amazing experience before I realized that the voice that spoke to me that day has always been in my head. It is the voice of a loving companion who used to comfort and watch me as a child, my own personal image of an inner guide.

So now, twenty years later, I feel that I understand something about the creative process that at times "turns up the heat" and accelerates our growth. Rather than waiting for a crisis, I have found that *aligning with your true heritage and your soul's original reason for incarnating here can become a daily spiritual practice*, one that will keep you on course, continually empowering you. Activating your desire to manifest your highest spiritual intent is what mythologist Joseph Campbell meant when he said that if we follow our bliss, doors will open. This alignment brings you a magical life—the kind that if you knew you were going to die tomorrow, you'd feel fulfilled and confident that you had completed what you came here for.

The process this book describes will serve you well if you are searching for a more purposeful way to live your life. As you learn in Part One, first you must align with your highest spiritual intention to manifest desired changes in yourself and discover your work in the world. Then, in Part Two, you are reminded of your bigger story—a kind of "double seeing" which connects this world with the greater one. With constant Self-remembrance, which is your natural way of being, your personal story can stay linked to the divine plan for humanity. In Part Three, you are shown practical ways to bring your spiritual future into your present life to help you better represent the human/Divine Self in this ordinary world. Specific directions for daily practices help bring these principles alive in your life as you travel the path.

Perhaps you are coming into the awareness that you are already a practical mystic. For truly, we are all mystics, awakening once more to our true powers as living souls. We need only to develop the eyes to see and the ears to hear to make this our reality.

PART ONE

THE POWER OF FOCUSED SPIRITUAL INTENTION

The most beautiful and most profound experience is the sensation of the mystical. It is the sower of all true science. He to whom this emotion is a stranger, who can no longer wonder and stand rapt in awe, is as good as dead.

—ALBERT EINSTEIN

GUIDES FOR HUMANITY

*Not those who busy themselves with speculations, with
social or "spiritual" activities, but only those who raise
themselves as high as heroic or ascetic experiences, go
further into the beyond.*

—JULIUS EVOLA, *Eros and the Mysteries of Love*

Throughout human history there have always
been key moments when many psychic cur-
rents run together and coalesce into a new
beginning for each of us. These points are marked by
some inner or outer "heroic event" in which our conscious and unconscious minds unite and change our
lives. We're coming to such a time right now, as we
journey forward into a new millennium. We see mas-
sive changes already starting to happen. Many of us are
poised, awaiting our next right step. A paradigm shift is
occurring; humanity's values are changing, and the
world as we've known it—politically, economically,
psychologically, religiously, and socially—is falling
away.

Here are some ways to describe this process: We're
having a spiritual awakening. We're undergoing an ini-

tiation. We're passing through a sequence of death and rebirth. We're committing "egocide" (not to be confused with suicide). We're taking a quantum leap in consciousness. And some of us feel we are simply going home. In other words, our consciousness is being "divinely tampered with."

But remember, we have free will. No higher consciousness can interfere with your personal life unless invited in. This would be a violation of spiritual law. Therefore, your *asking* is the key. Those who feel a response are part of a new group of world servers who rise to the call in every age and take the lead. These are the timeless mystics who clothe themselves in modern-day garb to fit into the current times. Practical mystics look like everybody else; the difference is that they envision the bigger picture. They know that what happens here is more than it appears to be. They are willing and able to serve as guides for others when called upon to do so.

In every age of human history certain people have felt a strong sense of destiny and realized there is something bigger going on here than meets the eye. These practical mystics are visionaries, but they are also grounded catalysts for change who know intuitively how to recognize and direct the natural process of personal and planetary transformation. They perform the sacred function of helping humanity evolve. Having already tapped into the core of the creative process, they know how to give spiritual principles a concrete expression to move us from the uncreated to the created. For they remember that they are divine. Because of their obvious strength of conviction and their faith in this process, these individuals are sought out by others for guidance and support. Though in the minority, these vision carriers hold steady with their unbending belief in the coming future while much else falls apart. These people haven't actually done anything to make their presence felt by others in this way; their authority is not a matter of *doing*, but of *being*.

A spontaneous flow of spirit naturally pours through their nature. And this spirit is contagious! When you are in the presence of such a person, you feel aligned with a higher purpose and can rest, content that everything is being guided by a Higher Power and that even your small life has a sacred meaning.

Practical mystics are guides for humanity during times of great change. They are the architects for the new era, for they can see the sacred within the ordinary world. They possess an intuitive understanding of how to die to the old and allow a Higher Order to make all things new. And they model this process for others, which is how they teach.

We ourselves are these artists and designers of the coming times, makers of the specific themes and events we intensely desire to experience. There appears to be a "universal fabric" or "cosmic soup" in which our consciousness is imbedded. This consciousness, our very life force, can be molded and visibly shaped into any type of matrix or design for every human potential we can imagine as a possibility. By using our creative imaginations, focused attention, and remarkable ability to create stories and assign meaning to things, we shape our reality. We do this in alignment with the Creative Force itself.

If we could draw a diagram of what is happening, we could see that our human will is merging with divine love itself. In so doing, we are cultivating qualities of courage, compassion, and understanding. We are aligning with the Creator's plan for humanity. Our prayer becomes:

For so it must be, and help me to do my part!

Are *you* one of these awakening ones, perhaps a "closet mystic" with an eye on the future life and ears to hear the inner instructions coming from your Source? If you are, you will know it.

THE MAGICAL WORK
OF FOCUSED INTENTION

*Truth never descends to our world of error; he who
would know it must ascend to that world of Reality
where he can see face to face and, for a while, become
living truth.*

—J. J. VAN DER LEEUW, *The Conquest of Illusion*

Practical mystics utilize the power of spiritual
intention through invocation and evocation.
You can learn to practice your highest spiritual
intention daily, and it will become the guiding principle that governs all your activities, in fact your whole
life. This will be not only for your sake, but for the
good of us all.

The practice of aligning with your spiritual intention every day focuses your energy and your interests
away from your past and toward your unfolding
future. It expands you beyond your personal life and
brings you face to face with a greater vision of reality.
In this new way of being, you may even choose to sacrifice some of your own happiness for the sake of
something with a higher purpose. Selfless service,
however, must come from a cup that is full, not empty.

7

Attempting to replace a needy ego's desires with selfless service to humanity does not work, because needy love isn't capable of being truly selfless. Sometimes, being seen as one who serves is the real motivation for service. The ego is attached to appearing "selfless." You may not be owning how much you need to be needed for your *own* self-esteem. If you are still carrying a heavy load of unexamined baggage from your past or sore places where you have been unable to forgive others, or yourself, these "uncooked seeds" may sprout up in your service relationships. Unfortunately, you might not even be aware of this. You will think your bad feelings are everyone else's fault!

Clarifying and focusing on your own true reason for being or doing anything is one of the simplest yet most profound ways to cut through fragmented truth. Seeing ourselves clearly is *active* meditation, or positive, forward-moving prayer. You build qualities, rather than reflecting upon them. Instead of stilling your mind, you are using it actively to build thought forms as a first step toward manifesting good works.

Allowing your focused spiritual intention to become a constant guide for all your earthly activities is more an attitude toward life than an actual technique. Though it begins with a specific activity, later it will become a way of life.

Here are some qualities that are prerequisites for the magical work of focused intention:

1. A respect for spiritual law and cosmic principle as the governing forces of reality.

2. An inner sensitivity to recognize your spiritual purpose and mission in life.

3. The ability to recognize spiritual law in action.

4. The capacity to overlook nonessentials and to emphasize essentials.

5. A willingness to voluntarily suppress your personal interests for the good of the whole.

6. A steady contact with an inner Source of wisdom, strength, and love.

7. A willingness to do your part whenever your divine assistance comes.

If you have these qualities, you are on your way to becoming a messenger of truth and love—a practical mystic. I've observed that when you commit to the process of putting God first, all your life circumstances begin fitting nicely with this goal. In my group work with hundreds of people each year who are coming into spiritual expression of their life's work, we use the following as our group invocation:

Let Reality govern my every thought and Truth be the heart of my life! For so it must be, and help me to do my part!

For us, *Reality* with a capital *R* means the Absolute Reality behind all our sense perceptions. The great psychologist Carl Gustav Jung called this *unus mundus*, or the "one world" that existed before us, containing all possible creations. By *Truth* with a capital *T*, we mean the Greater Truth behind all individual notions based on our idiosyncratic experiences.

Through your willingness to align with Reality and Truth you can invoke new qualities that counterbalance old weaknesses and immature or illusory aspects of your nature. In other words, you can count on this process to help you grow into the person you truly want to be, right now!

Your focused spiritual intent, when made conscious, gives you a way to emulate your greater Self right here, moment by moment, in your ordinary routines. It is an imitation process, in which you call up whomever or whatever it is that you desire to be. But once the new influences come, you must be willing to undergo whatever emotional, physical, and behavioral changes may be necessary for these purer qualities to come through. This is how we manifest heaven on earth. You are literally making yourself *transparent*, so you can shine forth the qualities of your higher Self with clarity. You are sculpting yourself into a bright instrument that matches the ideal in its essence. This is not a path for the fainthearted! You must be willing to remove or purify anything that is in the way of Truth.

The Power of Invocation

When the cry goes out, there is a response.

—Hermetic maxim

D ivine intervention awaits us at every turn of the cosmic wheel of destiny. A great principle or power lies behind every desired quality or possibility. All we have to do is petition it and then await the response.

Before we begin our actual practice, let's delve more deeply into this awesome power of calling forth a higher way and then living it.

Invocation is *active* prayer, cocreative prayer. It is self-assertive, will-to-action prayer that goes beyond traditional passive religious faith. Many think of it as the prayer for the coming age. In the past, we have prayed, but this has been an emotional appeal, more of a plea of helplessness, that a Higher Power come into our lives and do both its *and* our parts.

Invocation is how practical mystics pray, recognizing that we are cocreative, stating that we are ready and anxious to do our part. Knowing we don't have the power to create these high qualities and desired changes apart from our Creator, we invoke them and then make a commitment to enact them. This is a powerful commitment, and it requires the courage and conviction of a true adventurer, a seeker of wisdom, love, and dynamic spiritual will.

Invocation is a subtle, voiceless appeal, an *energetic* process that happens inwardly at certain points in our lives when we begin outgrowing attitudes and beliefs that no longer serve us. At these pivotal times, we freshen up our outworn doctrines and look for spiritual sustenance, a new way of life that speaks to our deeper nature.

According to psychologist Carl Jung, invocation is a concentration of psychic energy on a "God-image," a process which transfers the energy to the divine being or archetypal image constellated by our cry. Jung taught that archetypal beings appear spontaneously and have the power to act on their own, with an autonomy that is beyond our conscious mind's control. Therefore, it is not absurd to believe that when we cry out to a divine image that we envision, we will receive a response.

To cry out for change is part of our species' inherent urge to evolve, to expand our consciousness. Just as a plant reaches toward the sun, we humans are in movement toward Absolute Reality, seeking enlightenment, or whole Truth.

This yearning to transcend is innate in every species. Without it, no mineral would differentiate from earth, no plant would blossom or bear fruit, nor could any of us reach our full potential. This process of call and response, then, is the natural interplay between two dimensions of consciousness, causing a shift to a higher way. Just as a child extricates itself from parental influence, we humans as a species push toward transcending our material and mortal nature into divine life. Ultimately, this sacred hunger causes us to unite with our highest blueprint or ideal, bringing completion of the self.

Invocation is the call of our soul to awaken to a new and deeper aspect of our nature. This process is autonomous, coming from what Jung called the *collective unconscious mind*. This process is *a priori*, meaning it existed before we did! It's our built-in guarantee that we can *consciously* unite with our higher consciousness anytime we choose to enter upon this road less traveled.

To *invoke* means to "cry out," to seek a response from the appropriate inner guide or teacher from a higher consciousness. When we invoke a new quality or process, we seek to establish a new thought pattern. In plain language, we build inner strengths to meet the current and growing outer chaos. As we become good at this, we attract the people and experiences that will match this new and higher state.

Effort is required for the demanding work of personal transformation. But this kind of effort differs from the "ought tos" that feel like meaningless duties and obligations. It is an *inner* drive coming from our own Source, a voluntary striving and commitment to accelerate our path. We make a deliberate choice to be a conscious cocreator. Mystics of the world call this "stepping onto the path," or "following the Tao." It happens to those who are "in the fullness of time," when their turn to blossom arrives.

What do we do when we consciously invoke a Higher Order? How do we proceed? Well, the instructions are already within your powerful mind and heart, just awaiting your recognition and activation. The Daily Practices suggested in this book are only a reminder of what you already know of this process.

THE SCIENCE OF IMPRESSION

What is above form is called Tao; what is within form is called tool.

—RICHARD WILHELM, *I Ching*

In ancient Chinese philosophy there is a belief that the world arises from a preexistent image that comes into the Universal Mind. Then a copy manifests in our material world. Pattern is what regulates this process of imitation. The "seed" was divine. This is how any divine ideal takes shape in concrete reality.

An impression comes into our ordinary thoughts as a subtle reaction to some higher thought from a Higher Mind or group soul, of which we are all part. Sometimes it will come in as a whole concept or theme. This happens in our subjective life, though it may be stimulated by something we read in a book or hear in a lecture. We'll begin to dream about it, or perhaps we'll even become preoccupied with it. We might hear ourselves telling others we want this quality. Maybe we feel drawn to some creative endeavor, like a new career or artistic expression, or some new philosophy. It may even be something so new to us, we only have a glimmer of it, but for reasons we don't understand, this "something" now commands our attention.

Once I started dreaming of colored pencils—the expensive kind that come by the hundreds. I couldn't get them out of my mind. I started obsessing about them, feeling them in my hands, compulsively wanting to go buy a whole set—as a smoker feels about the urge for a cigarette. "This is ridiculous," I thought. "I'm not even an artist!" I told my business partner I wanted to buy a set of colored pencils. He was somewhat amused but agreed to add them to our company's purchase of supplies.

When I got home with the pencils, I couldn't wait to get to a piece of paper. I took out an art calendar for something to look at and put a pencil on the blank sheet. The first thing I drew was a fox's eye. It was so real, it stared back at me from the page! I was quite surprised, but I went ahead to draw a whole picture of a fox, freehand. And lo and behold, from this moment forward for the next six months, I couldn't stop drawing. I was indeed an artist. I couldn't believe how well I could draw (nor could my children or any of my friends)! After awhile, I'd made so many "perfect pictures," I became bored with the whole thing.

My Higher Self had taught me that we are all artists, which I believe was the whole purpose of this "cosmic impression" I experienced. I discovered that to be whatever we wish to be is simply a matter of having a very strong desire for something that completely captures our interest. Then we need the patience to create—which, of course, we won't have unless we are very attracted to the project. If you listen when a certain craving comes and *follow through* with it, you will be pleasantly surprised at how utterly talented you are—at anything!

This does not mean that you will manifest all these great spiritual gifts during your lifetime. After all, we are all living in finite bodies, and time limits where we can put our attention and resources. We can only follow what we feel is our path. For often, the study, practice, and experience required to manifest something in this time and space are quite consuming. This may explain why we are usually not vitally interested in too many things at once. Our interests usually move through cycles.

Yet, artist I am. And someday, when I'm not expending my energy on my work, I'll be delighted to once more pursue this God-given talent. Our commitment is the key that activates this process. We commit through our intention to "the work," and then the work enlightens us.

Any new creation starts as a vague interest, fascination, or desire impressed upon the mind. Where this impression comes from is a mystery. We know it is from some higher order than our ego can comprehend. Just as the colored pencils did to me, your impression will begin magically to call to you in whichever way it can get your attention. You might have a dream like I did. A great revelation could come in a flash, and you feel inspired.

Synchronicity could occur. For example, you

might dream something, mention it to a friend, then "by chance" run into someone or some opportunity that very afternoon that holds a key to pursuing this new interest. This is synchronicity in action, God's method of cause and effect. It's those events that seem to just drop in from nowhere that match something revealed in a dream, a revelation, or inner vision. Jung said these are times when there's a "rip in the fabric of ordinary reality" and we line up with the *unus mundus*, or Absolute Reality. Something bigger than life is being communicated from a deep source.

When you begin to receive something from beyond your ego's ordinary linear and logical thinking, like a synchronistic event, give it your reverent attention. This is the first step toward a new creation. It can be either fortune or misfortune, so be aware as it begins to unfold. If this is a seed that you do not wish to cultivate, you can nip it in the bud. If it contains some promise connected to your spiritual intention, you can help nurture its growth.

At first it will only be a vague impression. Then gradually it will slip into a definite thought form—which often comes in a flash. If the impression is coming from your highest good, it will be connected to your spiritual intention. If the thought is going to lead you off track—or into an unnecessary life lesson—it will be connected to your ego's desire nature, fueled by an unmet need. Examine your impressions carefully. Keep in mind that you can learn through *symbol* from your inner life, without having to act something out through a symptom in the world. Remember, the inner life holds the key to your transformation, and all does not have to be acted out through painful outer events.

In the next chapter, we take a look at the process of manifestation itself. Universal law governs this process, which will unfold in any form of new creation. From above downward into concrete reality, spirituality is brought into concrete form, and we are the implementors of this sacred work.

THE PROCESS OF MANIFESTATION

*The highest experiment is the experiment upon oneself
. . . Precisely in the offering of one's own spirit for the
sake of humanity is contained the sacrifice and the
acquisition. Each spiral, from above and below, will
appear as a circle, and every complication of the picture will vanish if we strive into the future.*

—AGNI YOGA

Manifestations begin as abstractions and enter
gradually into forms that can be seen, felt,
or experienced as "real" in this ordinary
world. It is the process of bringing spirit into materialization. We are all capable of performing this sacred
activity. Here is the natural process for anything
becoming "real-ized."

STEP 1

Intention. We intend that which we seek. We name
it and see it in our mind as a possibility. We *cry out* for
it. We are aligning our will with the will of our
Creator. And we are recognizing ourselves as cocreators. As the hands and feet of an abstract Spirit, we
have our part to do, too.

This is how something we want begins to take form. However, sometimes there is simply a flash of insight or a revelation about something we didn't know we were being given. These "answers" usually begin as surprises. They are holy, as they originate from beyond our ego. We were chosen to be their carriers.

STEP 2

Visualization. We note, with a deep commitment to truth and compassion for humanity, how this particular quality, thing, or event will be good for the whole. In this step we eliminate any selfish wish or request that could harm another. We make sure that we are "demonstrators of the Divine," serving both divine will as well as our own smaller purpose.

STEP 3

Projection. Once we are clear that our intention is good, we bring this ideal into our minds through our imagination, and we begin to more clearly formulate it. We picture it or see it happening in this world. We let our imagination play with it. We dream of it or have revelations around it. Sometimes this may shift or refine our original intention. During this process, any error in thought or any desire not in alignment with the good of the whole is weeded out.

STEP 4

Invocation. We bring all the love in our hearts for this ideal into our bodies and emotions. We deeply desire this dream or creation to come true. We let ourselves intensely feel our yearning and emotional desire for this manifestation. Human desire, when focused spiritually, is God's nature, which is love impressing our hearts.

In this step we are merging mind with heart. Both masculine and feminine principles are at work. The intensity of our desire for this new creation, our actual *felt experience* of it, will determine the potency of its coming into existence.

Sometimes during this stage you may realize you don't actually desire this thing enough, that you are following someone else's idea of what "should be" or representing some cause your own heart is not fully behind. Here you will meditate on this prospect and make certain it is what you want with all your heart.

STEP 5

Evocation. If you've determined that your mind and heart are in alignment, now your ego mind begins to form the actual ways and means for this new creation to become reality. Evocation always works together with invocation, as the response to the cry. You will draw a blueprint, form a committee, raise the money, buy the right supplies, bring together the craftspeople for this particular work—whatever is needed for it to become actual in our ordinary world.

STEP 6

Stabilization. You weed out all unrealistic, selfish,

impractical, or unusable parts of your divine plan. This is the time when many people become discouraged, but this stage is crucial to any good manifestation. Here, for instance, the architect might realize the builder cannot construct the house the way it was originally conceived, based on limitations of the site, finances, building codes, or other factors not anticipated.

At this stage, practical details are handled, the kind that are difficult for visionaries. Group work is often required here, for people tend to fall into two categories: some are excellent at thinking up new creations, but not so good at practical details or follow-through; others are better with the practical details than with conceiving or holding the vision. Both types are important for any sort of project, large or small, to become a reality.

STEP 7

Formulation. This is the culminating stage where the dream is actually built. The concrete activities are finished. All is worked out according to the plan, and all insight and forethought possible have now gone into the venture. Hopefully, this part will contain an impetus that can bring it all together.

Sometimes, at this point, a previously undetected error will be revealed. Some steps must be reviewed so any mistakes in the design can be eliminated or refined. You might even be working with the wrong craftspeople or with the wrong products or supplies.

This can be a test to make certain you really want this project to become a reality. This shouldn't shake your confidence in your pure intention. Often sacrifice is necessary on your part to let go of some attachment that may be impractical or not quite good enough for the whole. You simply need to look, perhaps at your own weaknesses or ignorance about some part of this, or communicate with your group in truthful cooperation. And then, you must have the patience and perseverance to go on.

Anytime you feel stuck, it's important to return to step 1, to remember your true spiritual intention. Then, the issue will often clear.

EXERCISE: DISCOVERING YOUR OWN PROCESS OF CREATION

Take some time to think back through your past and find an example of a wonderful creation you began, such as a new career, an artistic endeavor, a new relationship, or some particular project. Holding this creation in mind, take yourself through the stages above and see where what you did worked, or where it went wrong . . .

See what you can learn about how you go through the process of creation. We each have certain set patterns and fairly predictable ways of going off track, depending on our personality style and old ingrained habits . . . Be honest now, and see yourself clearly in this regard . . . Notice the qualities you have that need refinement, and name them . . . And see your valuable traits that carry you through, and name them . . .

As you ponder all this, see what your intuition shows you about your process—something that will allow you to remove some hindrances, to relax and be more creative. Ask your Higher Self to send you a revelation or a symbol showing you what you need to know right now to further your creative spiritual aspirations.

THE PRACTICE OF
SPIRITUAL INTENT

*One should not give up, neglect, or forget for a
moment his inner life, but he must learn to work in it,
with it, and out of it, so that the unity of his soul may
break out in all his activities.*

—MEISTER ECKHART

The process of creativity is often referred to as "magnetic work." You'll discover that your intention functions like an archetypal magnet, which draws to itself all that is required to formulate your spiritual ideal. This magnet follows Hegel's Law of Creativity, with its three arms:

- *thesis*—the new creation is conceived

- *antithesis*—the method of attainment is passed through

- *synthesis*—the statement of the new ideal is made real

In other words, we think up the new idea; then go through whatever is needed to be trained or made ready to receive the new qualities or skills. As the final stage, we take on the new, acting as the ideal in this world by being it. This dynamic three-part process reminds me of what Carl Jung said: "Man does not possess creative powers; he is possessed by them."

We always begin our new creation in the mind, through the use of our imagination. Right now, in your mind's eye envision a triangle, and put your intention, your new *thesis*, at the top. Now think about the process you will need to undergo to make this dream or creation a reality. Be warned that the stage of *antithesis* stirs up anything within you or in your life that cannot be contained in the new creation. This happens as our body/ego is purified to become a proper vessel for the simulation of the ideal you've called forth. So be careful what you choose to invoke.

For example, let's say you are invoking the quality of patience to balance an overly impetuous nature. During the antithesis phase, you will be showered by opportunities that try your patience to the hilt while your impetuousness is being refined. You will be required to practice patience until it becomes natural to you.

It helps to remember that your highest spiritual intention is to evolve—to sweep clean those dusty corners of your psyche and life that are impediments to your growth. Instead of running away when the going gets rough, listen inwardly and stay dead-honest with yourself. Then do what must be done.

Moreover, if you are intent on manifesting Spirit, you must be willing to put a daily spiritual practice in place. Each morning, reaffirm your vision so that the fabric that's been woven on the inner side will not be rent.

The key, then, for the ascension of our consciousness into the expanded, clear reality into which we're moving lies in our ability to hold steady with our highest spiritual intent while we undergo the daily ups and downs of ordinary life. Especially if you are in a transformational cycle, your road may be rocky at times, and it's easy to become discouraged, overwhelmed, or trapped, forgetting the overview.

For example, you may be confronted by a friend or relative about one of your character traits. You become angry and defensive, and your tendency is to justify yourself and walk away. This is the nongrowth stance. Remember that your highest spiritual intention is to evolve. Instead of running away, you'll need to really listen and gain self-knowledge so you can grow.

A reminder: Just as an outside expert cannot "fix" us as though we were a piece of equipment, neither can the Higher Self just reach down and "fix" us, unless we willingly comply. We've seen now that invoking is not sitting around doing mental affirmations: *Invoking it is doing it!* This eventually leads to being it. This is the cocreative process in action.

The fires of inspiration enter our minds and hearts when we invoke a new quality. All acts of creation are sacred, utilizing the three processes of *experiment*, *experience*, and *expression*. In other words, it is *by*, *through*, and *as* the One Self that we are continually made new. Some people call this "soul-making."

If, for example, you decide to marry, you start out with the prospect of your ideal marriage as your thesis. Then, your ego mind takes hold of the idea and shapes it into its perceptions of what an ideal marriage is: *Your spouse will love you dearly and never criticize you. You will always feel deeply in love.*

Then, reality sets in. And you go through the disillusionment of an imperfect situation and an oh-so-human mate (*antithesis*). So you accept your fate and start to adjust. (Or, maybe you abandon the project, unable to match your ideals with the sometimes unpleasant details and imperfections of real marriage.)

But finally, some result is seen—the "entity" that you two together have made comes to life. When anything reaches *synthesis*, it just is. Now, the creative energies have settled, and nothing new is occurring. This can lead to a feeling of resolution. But the danger is stagnation.

As the clay is provided for the potter, we are given the *prima materia*, the raw material, from which we evolve ourselves into higher and higher forms. God provides the clay; we are the meaning-givers, assigning our lives and all their contents their definition by our perceptions and the meanings we attach to them. This is our part in the cocreative process.

WHEN THE THREE BECOME FOUR

For something to take form, a foundation must be built; that being so, the Three become the Four.

—HERMETIC PRINCIPLE

The divine triangle of creativity is a magnetic field of three energies—thesis, antithesis, and synthesis, but it is not in form. All creative processes begin in the mind. When a cosmic law formulates in our lives, however, it fulfills the metaphysical maxim: "the three become four."

Just as a pyramid seems to be a triangular structure until you view it from the top and see that its foundation is a square, when the three becomes four, a foundation is built in the concrete world for a new creation to take form. Now these dynamic superhuman energies shift into ordinary human activities.

There are four directions, four archangels who stand guard at the four corners, four winds, four temperaments, four seasons. In the building blocks of any new creation, we flow through four distinct functions:

1. RECEPTION

You will begin to receive thoughts about whatever you are creating. If you get a negative thought, or one that is harmful in any way, you can defocus and let it die of inattention. If it is a desired creation, an *experiment* is being set up by your focus and attraction, and you will begin to receive further thoughts about what is coming into being.

At first, these thoughts will accumulate around what your ego thinks it knows about such matters, basing these concepts on perceptions of past experiences and fantasies. If we are full of misconceptions, the experiment will become tainted by these delusions.

2. ASSIMILATION

The *experience* of whatever you are creating in the outer world is initiated at this stage. Through experiencing the ups and downs of our thesis, we learn, and as we do, we hone our creation. Whatever error or faulty vision we may be operating under is refined at this stage through the crucible of experience in our daily routine.

The Higher Self and the shadow struggle through this stage. But through love, acceptance, inner dialogue, and making all negative aspects conscious, the ways of your darker side can eventually be refined to match the Higher Self's ways. This refinement will happen through the pain of failure, negativity, disillusionment, or sometimes humiliation. But hopefully, you will also be assimilating the Higher Self's strengths to offset some of this ordeal.

3. TRANSMUTATION

This part of the purification process elevates your lower urges or ideas to a higher plane. Something has corrected itself through exposure to a higher idea or experience. Death and rebirth have taken place. The positive ego and the Higher Self bring about this stage.

When any part of ourselves becomes hardened in the coverings of egoism, it is consumed in the "fire" of transmutation. If we cannot get the point through our inner psychological work, symbolic visions, or dreams, the Self will set up a crisis in our outer life. This crisis can sometimes bring us to our knees, so we will come out of denial and look our error squarely in the face.

4. EXPRESSION

In this stage the new creation is *lived*—radiating naturally from our heart's desire and transmitted through our transformed way of thinking. Expression is our service to humanity. The new creation is now being *stated* in the world, perceived as *fact*. It is showing through us, as *us*. All three aspects of the Self have integrated around whatever you were learning about or making conscious. Now the experiment is a *fait accompli*.

EXERCISE: COCREATING

Take some time now to study the four functions of creativity: reception, assimilation, transmutation, and expression. Then see which of these you are naturally inclined toward, and note the stages where you may stumble, hurriedly pass through, or be unskilled.

Then, commit to make conscious your weaknesses and practice your unloved parts. Some people are great at envisioning new things, for example, but not so good at nurturing them, allowing them to mature. Others may never try to be creative, believing themselves to be are dull and unimaginative.

If you are great at taking another's lead and patiently nurturing a project, but believe you are not creative, perhaps now is a good time to correct this misconception. For creativity is a universal human/divine process available to us all. No one is exempt from being a cocreator!

DAILY PRACTICES

Practical life is not separate from religious exercises. Religion isn't for Sunday or for Friday night; it is for all day, every day . . . It's through life that one is to experience the spirit, can communicate the spirit, and live the spirit.

—JOSEPH CAMPBELL

I f you are ready to proceed beyond an intellectual understanding of this process, the following exercises will teach you experientially what you need to know. You can use this process as a prototype for any type of invocation you may choose to call forth.

EXERCISE: INVOKING AN IDEAL MODEL

Use this exercise to get in touch with the Higher Self, or some other Ideal Model needed to integrate the personality or achieve desired behavior.

Take some time to go into a relaxed state. Then close your eyes and visualize yourself walking down a corridor of a museum, slowly approaching a statue that is emerging in the distance. Allow the images to come spontaneously.

As you are approaching this statue, you are beginning to see its form emerge, and you realize it is an image of the Ideal Self that you seek.

Be aware of what this image looks like in as much detail as you can envision, its stance . . . the expression on its face . . . its attire . . . Experience the essence of this being for a moment . . . Discover how you feel in its presence.

For the next few minutes, just let yourself experience a relationship with this being . . . (take a long pause) Now, slowly move toward this being, allowing yourself to come closer . . . and closer . . . staying in touch with how you feel . . .

Now, merge with this ideal image . . . You are coming down off the pedestal and moving around the room . . . You are walking in its feet, moving its arms and legs, breathing its breath . . . You are being this divine one.

Stay with this image for awhile now, taking on all its qualities . . . Feel them entering into your heart and mind . . . (long pause)

Now, gradually allow this image to separate from you, going back to its pedestal, becoming a statue once more . . . Notice how you feel as the two of you separate . . .

And just before it becomes immobile once more, this divine being reaches down and gives you a gift to place in your heart . . . something to remember it by. Accept this gift now . . . and place it in your heart . . . Notice how it feels to be the bearer of this symbol or gift . . . (long pause)

Take some time to thank your Ideal Model, and then gradually experience this inner scene fading into a light gray mist as you feel yourself coming back into your ordinary waking state of consciousness once more . . . and open your eyes.

Take some time to reflect on this experience. You may want to write, meditate, or draw for awhile.

In processing this experience, pay particular attention to who or what this Image seemed to be, its essential qualities, and how it felt to be this Ideal. Discover what all this means for you right now in your daily life.

EXERCISE: INVOKING
A POSITIVE QUALITY

Use this exercise when you seem stuck in a negative way of behaving, feeling, or thinking and want to open up to a new possibility.

First, clearly define the negative quality you are seeking to transform. For example, let's say it is extravagance. Let the feeling of extravagance come forth, and feel it completely. Discover its essential nature.

Now, contemplate what the opposite of this trait would be and name it For example, let's say it is Simplicity. (Remember though, no one can assign you this opposite quality; you must come up with this yourself.)

The essence of Simplicity, an archetype, must now be planted in your consciousness, preparing to manifest. Close your eyes for a moment, and see this happening in your mind . . .

Take some time to meditate on this new quality and feel it entering into your mind . . . your emotional body . . . and now your physical body . . . Become Simplicity!

As Simplicity, let yourself turn into a symbol of this divine quality . . . Take whatever comes in spontaneously, and place it in your heart . . .

Now, let the symbol speak to you from within your own mind and heart . . .

Once you feel your focus is exact and the message is clear, begin to imagine yourself walking around during a day in your ordinary life utilizing this quality . . . See what happens . . .

Now, slowly, still retaining all that goes on inside, simultaneously be aware that you are right here in this world . . . Open your eyes and come fully back into the room where you are sitting. You may want to reflect for awhile, write something, or draw a picture.

For your aid in this practice, here are some of the ideal qualities that have emerged most often from persons using this technique:

Acceptance, Appreciation, Authenticity

Beauty, Being, Belonging

Calmness, Centeredness, Childlikeness
Compassion Comradeship, Concreteness
Courage, Creativity, Curiosity
Daring, Decisiveness, Detachment
Determination, Discipline, Discretion
Ease, Empathy, Endurance, Enthusiasm
Faith, Freedom, Friendliness
Generosity, Genuineness
Goodheartedness, Grace
Harmlessness, Harmony, Humility, Humor
Initiative, Integration, Integrity
Leadership, Light, Love
Mutuality, Nonattachment, Order
Patience, Peacefulness, Persistence
Position, Positiveness, Power, Purity
Reality, Respondability, Responsibility
Serenity, Service, Significance
Silence, Simplicity, Stability, Synthesis
Thoughtfulness, Tolerance, Trust, Truth
Understanding, Unity, Vitality
Wholeness, Will, Wisdom, Wonder

To add potency to taking on any new quality or behavior, here are a few suggestions:

1. Begin talking about this new aspect of yourself to your friends, declaring your intent to develop it in your character. This grounds the thought in reality, giving the unconscious mind a chance to believe it and to cause it to happen.

2. Begin acting as if you possess this quality—imagine the archetype Simplicity overshadowing you, doing things that represent its nature. You will find yourself behaving differently, as if by magic. This really works!

3. Write the word Simplicity everyday for a while, placing it somewhere in your room where you can see it, to be reminded of it. Or draw a picture of its symbol, keeping it close by.

EXERCISE: INVOKING A SYMBOL

Symbols are couriers of consciousness, mediators between the created and the uncreated worlds. They are carriers of meaning and transformational energy. In a way, they can serve as shortcuts to the achievement of your spiritual aims.

For example, I may seek to invoke the quality Strength or Courage while I perform some major task. I can call the quality down and begin to emulate it. To help strengthen this transmutation process, I can ask for a symbol to be placed in my mind or heart, representative of this desired quality.

Here's a way to try this powerful technique:

Sit quietly, just for a moment or two, and focus inward. Then, concentrate with all your might on what you're seeking . . . and move into the essence of it. To move into the essence of something, you imagine it with all your might—what it feels like to be it, its texture, its structure, all its ways. Then, focus on clothing yourself in this quality. Qualities usually enter into your heart from some deep well within. You can feel this happening. If you want a symbol to carry around with you for a more concrete union, ask for one. Then, sit and wait. In a few minutes, it will come.

Accept whatever comes first. A divinely given symbol shouldn't be tampered with by your ego. Saying, "Oh, I don't want it to be this symbol; I'd rather it be such and such" is not creative; it's the ego giving you something you already know—something from your past. Rather, you are calling forth a new quality, something never before realized by you. So you must take what comes spontaneously and then learn from it as it becomes a part of you and teaches you its ways.

The archetype of Courage, for instance, was recently sent to me symbolically as elongated wings, graceful and flowing. I was somewhat taken aback, as I've not thought of angel wings as being a necessary symbol for Courage. But as I reflected upon this divine image, it became very clear to me these were the wings of St. Michael. And since he carries a sword and is known for "fighting dragons," this indeed began to make sense. If I don these wings in my imagination, I can simulate the quality of Strength this patterning represents. In my mind, I am empowered by this blessed archangel, the archetype of the Spiritual Warrior.

A symbol of something you imagine comes from the abstract world of the uncreated and the formless. With meaning, you have dressed it in form. It enters into your ego mind, which has the power to interpret this symbol in its own special manner. The individual meaning you give it links this supraordinary power with this ordinary concrete world. Now it has meaning in two worlds at once and can, therefore, serve as a bridge, opening these two disparate realities to each other. Once this bridge is built between your abstract (spiritual) mind and your concrete (earthly) intellect, you can "walk across" into the higher dimension and gain a greater understanding of any aspect of your life. You may not know which quality you need for some human project. You may go into your abstract spiritual mind completely unfettered and let the Higher Order choose what you need. You can enter in complete surrender.

We can take charge and see, through symbol and inner vision, what we desire. Then, we assert our plea and await the response. Let me give you an example: I call out for a symbol to give me a higher understanding of some issue. I sit quietly, close my eyes, and go inward. Then slowly, from my inner field of awareness, an image spontaneously appears of an Indigo Blue Sword in a Red Leather

Holder. All this, including the colors, will have both a personal and a universal meaning. I look for the personal first: What does this symbol mean to me?

A Sword means personal power, courage, and protection. Indigo Blue is the energy of Love and Wisdom, very rich and deep, my Source. Red is the dynamic life force itself—our life's blood, dangerous, but earthy and strong. Red is also spiritual will, with an arrow-like directive energy that can destroy the old for the sake of a bigger truth.

I interpret this as my coming into power as a Spiritual Warrioress. I see the goddess Athena briefly; then, she changes into the Queen of Swords from the tarot deck, who leads a procession holding a sword upright, looking straight ahead. She represents the ability to "cut through the illusions of the mind."

So now, with a blending of universal meaning applied to my individual understanding, I have my "reply." My task now will be to apply all this inner knowledge to my personal life in concrete ways. For without the practical aspect, these higher truths are irrelevant. If, however, our spiritual intention is well thought out and we are fully committed to living it, to putting our whole self—our time, interest, mental validation, feelings, and actions—behind our sacred and highest intention, we'll hold strongly on course, whether passing through pleasure or pain.

BRINGING THE SACRED
INTO THE ORDINARY

There is a deep purpose in Nature which is the self-unfoldment of all things, of the hidden nature in them. In this unfoldment there is joy, there is creation, there is beauty.

—SRI RAM

Life's usual predicaments take so much out of us and cause us to become so fragmented, it's important to realize that our spiritual intention will always bring us back to our senses anytime we feel tossed about by fate.

If, for example, my spiritual intention is to grow and evolve, I know I can undergo whatever temporary sadness, conflict, or even relational confrontation that may be necessary for my growth and evolution to proceed. My intention will give me courage, even substance, as I undergo the trials that must occur for me to be whole.

Here are some examples of spiritual intentions large enough to contain our wholeness. Use them to guide you in formulating your own intention to hold your sacred purpose in place:

- I am here to fulfill God's plan for my life.

- I am here to manifest heaven on earth.

- I am here as a representative from a Higher Order that is benevolent and works for the good of the earth and all its peoples.

- I am here as a Spiritual Warrior.

- I am here to become more loving.

- I came here as a communicator of wisdom and love.

- I am to serve as a bridge between two worlds.

- I am here to develop my creative talents to share with the world.

- I've come to this planet to help with the transition to the new millennium.

- I am here to be a good householder and learn to be a good partner and parent.

When I hold firm to a spiritual intention, I can see that whatever happens in the outer world that makes me more courageous, compassionate, or understanding will have a sacred purpose for my life. I can spiritualize all my activities in this manner.

On the other hand, if my intention is always to be happy, or if I equate material possessions with happiness—you can see where this could lead. It would mean I would always be striving for this happiness or material wealth, perhaps even at another's expense—and certainly at my own. I would be convinced I am a failure in life if I don't achieve total happiness or high financial success. And since life automatically contains both success and failure, pain and pleasure, sickness and health, life and death, I will find no gratification. I'm setting myself up to be a failure if I pursue some unrealistic goal my ego may crave—when, in fact, it's all an illusion. We must learn to accept it all as good, and see the beautiful and sacred in it all, no matter what.

So I must be willing to have a big enough intention to take in life's dualities, both the shadow and the light, the high times and the low. For this is just how life is and how fulfillment really comes. To take on a superficial intention, such as "I'm here to gratify my needs" or "My purpose is always to be young," will eventually bring disaster. These limited goals come from an ego-driven personality, not imbued with spiritual force at all.

Our creative minds, our intuition, and our dreams can make new creations. We can even decide all together to create a whole new world where the sacred is once more honored! Theosophist C. W. Leadbeater expressed the magical power of intention in these eloquent words:

We have only to think strongly of an idea, and that which ensouls it or represents it will manifest itself to us. Any strong thought of devotion brings an instant response; the Universe would be dead if it did not.

Knowing we have this power and this divine right, our true task, then is to

1. Remember that thought is creative.
2. Create what we want with clear intention-through our powerful active imaginations.

3. Stick with the original intent and our highest ideals, no matter how we might struggle through the ordeals of any new formulation.

4. Recognize and work with whatever comes when we invoke our deepest spiritual desires.

5. When something is finished, let go and move on toward what is unfolding.

6. Strive to become effortless "demonstrators of the divine."

When we choose to invoke something from a Higher Order, we are taking a stand as cocreators in the divine plan and giving our lives a sacred purpose. We can either do this consciously now and awaken, or unconsciously, as we've done in the past. But participate we must! So we may as well take responsibility for our part and not simply throw ourselves haphazardly into the spirals of fate.

The soul is big! It treks through its "grades in school" spread out over many lifetimes—from the beginning of time until now—always unfolding, always taking on life afresh, in every generation. You don't have to believe in reincarnation to know this. Our DNA is a "time traveler," having been us since time began. So you can consider this scientifically, through the generations in your family chain if you so choose.

But the important thing is not to miss what is happening in your very essence. You came here on purpose. And your life counts for something grand—though much of it seems to pass you right by. It helps, of course, to have traveling companions, lovers, friends, and teachers along the way. But the real work is within you! You are an amazing work of art—so beautiful a design that God actually made you utterly unique.

It's important to honor yourself for your courage, understanding, and growing compassion as you mature into your whole Self. And never forget that you are both human and divine—a member of a true "hybrid species" at this particular stage in your unfolding—on your way to full blossoming. It's up to each of us what type of future we wish to cocreate and then share with one another in harmony and delight. For anything is possible when we can believe it, invoke it, recognize it, and then make it so.

Our only qualification is that we must know exactly what we wish to create, because if we focus intently upon something, it *will* manifest in some fashion in our lives. When we are willing to take on life fully, as many of the great Beings who came before us have done, we fall into our natural state as cocreators, which is bliss. Then all our suffering ceases. This does not mean we won't still experience times of pain or distress with our times of pleasure: the complementary opposites are both real and essential to keep us "on the mark." But pain and pleasure are mere states of consciousness, intense experiences that can be entered into and not feared at all. Suffering, however, is another thing. It is the failure to let go of something that's no longer working. It is holding on to the past. Suffering takes us into victimhood and feelings of powerlessness over our lives. And this is the opposite of the practical mystic's way.

Trusting our native instincts and following our bliss is an actual felt experience in which we learn to reside on a higher frequency than that of our ego's worrisome life. We shift our focus inwardly and take on the life of our ideal, where a sense of meaning and sacred purpose abound. In this way, we participate in our own creation story.

A great big door may have opened for you now, as it has done for me. For once you empower your own abilities as a cocreator, your life becomes magically imbued with Spirit. From now on, you'll feel guided every step of the way, for you'll be "on line," doing your part. And never again will you be without a deep connection to your own Source, who is all-knowing and divine.

GUIDED IMAGERY:
TODAY'S PRACTICAL MYSTIC

To ground you in your new awareness of your power as a practical mystic, sit quietly and allow your creative imagination to take you on a mystic's journey:

With your inner eye, see yourself walking along a path that leads into the future. Just ahead is a long line of advanced souls who have traveled this earthly existence for a long, long while, seasoned in the ways of this world and beyond. You follow along, knowing that you, too, are a part of this lineage . . .(pause to take in this realization)

As you move along the path, you become aware that there is more darkness behind you, and more light as you progress . . . And you reflect on all the knowledge and experience you gained from your time here on earth. Allow images of whatever memories arise now to come fully into your interior view . . . See the joys . . . the disappointments . . . the illusions that held you in their sway . . . (long pause) Acknowledge the relationships that were especially significant for you with gratitude and a deep sense of reverence for the gift they each gave you . . . (pause)

Now, experience yourself "seeing double," seeing your old life behind you while simultaneously getting a flavor of your life just ahead, and knowing that you are now between these two states of being . . . (pause)

Feel yourself as both the personality named (insert your name) and your soul . . . and simultaneously hold these two states of being together as one Self . . . (long pause)

See yourself following along now, into a new vibratory field, with head held high, and a deep sense of contentment and faith in the process . . . (pause)

Now, still retaining all that just happened inwardly, come back to this reality and take some time to reflect and process the felt awareness or insights that come up. You may want to write in your journal or draw about this experience.

Part Two

The Practice of
Self-Remembrance

Do not think carnally, or you will be flesh, but
think symbolically, and then you will be Spirit.
—John 3:3-7, as interpreted by Carl Jung

STEPPING INTO YOUR GREATER IDENTITY

What, on a lower level, had led to the wildest conflicts and to panicky outbursts of emotion, now looks like a storm in the valley seen from the mountain top. This does not mean that the storm is robbed of its reality, but instead of being in it, one is above it.

—CARL GUSTAV JUNG, *Alchemical Studies*

At the center of your consciousness, like the nucleus of a cell, lives a "spark of mind" representing your grand design, a core Self who never leaves. This bigger You is who you really are, a wise Self who can think clearly beyond all the twists and turns you travel in your ordinary life. We've not been taught much about this inner knower, which can hold the vision even in the midst of our wildest conflicts and panicky outbursts. This part of you feels compassion for all humanity, so its motivations are always pure and harmless. It is a fair witness consciousness, keyed to your greater life unfolding on a larger canvas.

Your true Self's function is to nudge you gently back onto your path anytime you lose touch with your highest intentions. You can fulfill your purpose here and now, for our time of completion has come. Humanity is about to move into a whole new consciousness. But as we end this millennium and begin a whole new era of human history, many are still sleeping, not the least prepared for this awesome event!

We've all spent time looking back at who we've been. But unfortunately, when we constantly view ourselves through a rearview mirror, we lose touch with our potential. We don't have an image of our greater identity. Instead, we're constantly reacting to our past, and this distorts our present interactions. As Oprah Winfrey, having noted this pattern again and again in the people she interviews, asks, "We all see now that we're from dysfunctional homes. So what are we going to do about it?" Most people haven't yet realized that we need to turn in a whole new direction to move ahead. *We are the meaning-makers of our lives.* Whatever we focus on and give meaning to becomes our reality.

Mythologist Joseph Campbell once said that we'd better have a great big story, or no story at all. It's getting caught up in all those middle-sized stories that causes so much trouble. When you can see your Bigger Story through a wider lens, you become conscious of larger patterns and story lines that may have kept you hooked into your past.

You might think of this section of the book as your instruction guide for turning inward and reconnecting with your *real* story, the one that's unfolding in the much larger framework of your subjective inner life.

It's here in this "soul-sized" life that your true ideals take shape.

To move beyond where you are, you'll need a new definition for yourself. Little has been taught to us about our *greater* side, this magnificent potential Self—the Self which represents your highest expression as a soul in human form. That's certainly worthy of your recognition, wouldn't you say?

Your greater Self wills your actions through two main qualities, Wisdom and Love. What you think with your mind and feel in your heart is ultimately who you become. As Jesus said, "As a man thinketh in his heart, so is he."

As you read, you'll become reacquainted with these two aspects of your nature that are living through you from inside. And, perhaps, if you are somewhat out of balance here—too cerebral and detached, or too emotional and attached—you may find yourself more balanced. For the Middle Way is the key to peace of mind. It's from the midpoint, not the extremes, that we learn to be *in the world, but not of it.*

Your Bigger Story is part of a divine plan; therefore, it has archetypal significance. Archetypes are humanity's divine ideals. These are the blueprints we're growing into. When your time of completion comes, you'll blossom fully into your whole design.

A female client once told me how she used this principle in her life—without even realizing it. She had been dreaming for weeks about being a woman of great wisdom and beauty, dedicated to service. She saw herself helping others as they struggled with their various human predicaments in vignettes that looked like movie scenes. I asked her actually to become this Wise Woman in her ordinary life, to act "as if" for several weeks. One day she came for her session so radiant I hardly recognized her. She'd seen herself in the mirror that morning as the woman she'd so greatly admired. She had incarnated this beautiful, wise self-image.

Our main task, then, while in human form, is to be forever willing to interpret our life story within its greater sacred purpose. Then we'll take on our true spiritual identities.

In terms of seeing this bigger picture, the philosopher Arthur Schopenhauer suggested this analogy:

Life may be compared to a piece of embroidery of which, during the first half of our time, we get a sight of the right side, and during the second half of the wrong. The wrong side is not as pretty . . . but it is more instructive; it shows the way in which the threads have been worked together [to make the pattern].

In these pages you'll meet your most reliable guides for showing you the wrong side of your tapestry, your wise inner knower and your compassionate heart. These divine ideals hold the key.

All of humanity is passing over a threshold now into a new dimension. This will require a shift in our *perspective*—a transformation in mind. Once we understand, we can shift perspective in the twinkling of an eye. When you identify with these higher principles, you'll feel inspired with spiritual intent. You will claim your full powers as a human being and be able to rise quite effortlessly to the next place in your evolution. This new being you're becoming is moving into an entirely different world, a world in harmony.

And you may be one of those who are choosing to wake up and go first. But before you can transcend your old self, you must recognize the principles of your higher life with an attitude of complete sincerity and willingness to do your part. You must abide by certain rules of the road. Your sincerity and willingness are powers that bring you closer to your highest spiritual intentions. Use these well, and you will evolve rapidly along this accelerated path, familiar to the mystics of every age. When you can function more from the higher principles, all else falls into place.

Consciously choosing to evolve sets you apart. All of nature is evolving, of course, but most people just allow nature to take its course, not really wanting to take on spiritual evolution as a conscious activity. You can feel this resistance in many people, maybe in some of the people closest to you; it's even in society's institutions. If you are one who chooses the accelerated path, you won't be in the majority, but you will make the new life a reality. Your mission is sacred. It is a vital function for humanity as a whole.

You'll find the transformational journey is not for the fainthearted! Inviting your whole self into your conscious life changes you—forever. It brings you from unconscious to conscious living. Be sure you're willing, for you may never again look at your life in the same old familiar way. Your Higher Mind and Heart will bring a whole new perspective to your personal life.

I hope what follows validates what you already instinctively know in the depths of your soul and gives you exactly what you need to make your transformation.

GREAT CHANGES ARE IN STORE!

It is the worst thing when people do not know how to escape from the old rut. It is dreadful when they approach new conditions with their old habits. Just as it is impossible to open a present-day lock with a medieval key, likewise it is impossible for people with old habits to unlock the door of the future.

—AGNI YOGA TEACHINGS INFINITY, VOL. II

We look around us and see that much of what we've taken for granted is shifting before our eyes. Much dogma that we'd accepted without question—beliefs we'd bought into because "they" said so—is peeling off and crumbling into ash, along with many of our taken-for-granted idols and ideals. Our identities are being smashed and our self-concepts fragmented.

The discontent about their lives that so many people are expressing today is often tinged with a sense that long-held preconceptions are dissolving. I've heard statements like these a lot lately:

• I want to live more simply so I can pursue my real life's work.

61

- More money doesn't do it for me anymore.
- I feel like my life force is drying up. It's time to get rejuiced.
- Everything just fell apart while I was going merrily along. But it seems to be some kind of gift.
- Another great lesson has been resolved, and now I'm moving on.

Some people believe the critical mass that will move humanity forward to its next evolutionary stage has been reached, and we're all about to change—want to or not. Our search for personal meaning and soul fulfillment is a sign of this coming transition, right out where everyone can see it.

In the midst of outer confusion and disillusionment, you may be responding to an inner call to awaken and live more attuned to the real essentials in your life. You may feel an urgency to align with something greater than you are, and may share the sense that if you do not, we humans as a species may not survive.

Many of us have believed all along that we were just living our own lives. Our robotlike day-in, day-out routines make it seem this way. But now, we may be sensing that a *Greater Life just might be living us!*

We each make up this cocreative process as we go along. *For we are Self-evolving organisms.* An old story tells of a "wingless bird"—a symbol for humanity's present condition—which has been trapped in its plight for so long that it has forgotten how to fly. When the time is right, a "winged bird" with visionary powers arrives and attaches itself to the wingless bird, teaching it new skills, merging its essence with it, and ultimately leading it back to the freedom of flight. This ability to merge with something higher is part of the human story as well. It is the transcendence that takes us to the next level of soul growth.

The perennial philosophy describes this movement up the evolutionary ladder as the spiritual history of the soul's life, unfolding into the cosmic flow. Metaphysics, astronomy, archaeology, astrophysics, cosmology, spiritual psychology, and the mystical paths of both East and West all teach of this greater life. They call it the "science of the soul." You become part of this greater life as you learn to demonstrate divine principles. Our own direct knowledge is a "scientific library" of the bigger, soul-sized facts that can steady us while our egos "die."

A new millennium is dawning. A new way of knowing our God-nature is being revealed to us right now. In the age that is now passing we learned devotion and how to worship a transcendent outer God. Now we're turning inward and learning of the immanent God, "the God-within all of nature," including our own. When we recognize that the Divine lives inside our own nature, we become capable of masterful expression. This is a transformative insight, but it's also a huge responsibility.

We must begin by resolving our psychological issues. We need to make the emotional distortions that rule our spiritual lives conscious before we can assume our real spiritual identities.

This is where the Observer Self comes in. This Observer part of us is not caught up in the chaos of our emotional lives; it sees the bigger picture. Understanding our experiences through the larger context of each predicament we face, we begin to build inner strength.

The Observer Self is not just a subjective psychological reality, however; it is a scientific fact. Modern physics has discovered that until we make an observation, our consciousness is not attracted to anything and does not create anything. Everything stays in the background, as an undifferentiated field of movement and energy. Science has concluded that there is no reality except what we choose to observe and call "real." Physicist Fred Alan Wolf says the manner in which we perceive things is determining our lives: "The how of it determines the what of it."

PARTICIPATING CONSCIOUSLY IN YOUR OWN CREATION

The aim of the evolutionary process is to create a more noble, more sober, more far-seeing, more sensitive, more compassionate, and more loving individual . . . Those who think their spiritual discipline has come to fruition would do well to assess their progress by a critical examination of their own thoughts and behavior to know how far their evolution conforms to the standards set in the great religious scriptures of the world.
—GOPI KRISHNA, *Kundalini for the New Age*

We can see from the "bird's-eye view" that renewal is our constant activity; that is, if we are willing to accept life's challenges with an adventuresome spirit, willing to become involved with integrity in whatever crosses our path.

Your soul-making process naturally unfolds within you in the form of sequences of dying to the lesser life to make room for the greater one that is always evolving. This process is not a *physical* death; it is a constant flow through life, dying to the old and being reborn to the new, all in your current body!

Some rebirths are preceded by small deaths, when we've died to something that just wasn't very important to us, like a casual friendship, a possession, an idea. Others, however, can be huge and may even require professional help. For example, we might experience the death of a major role or aspect of our life that we felt we needed, like the loss of a significant relationship that nurtured us or a job that gave us our financial support.

This unrelenting movement toward wholeness is the working of a human "individuation" that culminates in our blossoming into completion. The great psychologist Carl Jung spent most of his life studying and writing about this process. To *individuate* means "to become an indivisible whole, no longer capable of being divided." This process is universal. It's how we humans move from fragmentation to wholeness. It is the work of "soul-making," the shift from being ego-dominated to allowing a greater spiritual identity to come in and spontaneously guide our life.

Can you imagine yourself as completely dominated by the urges of your soul, no longer needy as an ego? Think about it for a minute. What image do you see?

Moving into greater and greater identity through the process of individuation is moving perpetually in the direction of more and more freedom. If we consciously choose to develop, we continue to attract new possibilities that enrich our lives. If we remain unconscious participators in life, however, we tend to attract the same old lessons to ourselves, *ad nauseam*! The actors or the costumes may change, even the geography, but the issues remain unchanged, and we do not evolve or grow.

For each of us, and for humanity as a whole, individuation is the soul's maturation. This maturation maximizes the development of our unique personalities. Eventually we each merge back into the archetypal Self—humanity as one Soul. From the Self we originate, and to the Self we return when complete.

EXERCISE: DISCOVERING YOUR SELF-IDENTITY

Before going any further in your Self-exploration, stop for a moment and reflect on how you identify yourself. Who do you think you are? If I were to ask you right now, "Who are you?" what would you reply? For a great Self-awareness exercise, stop right now and write down ten endings to the phrase "I am . . ."

Now take some time to reflect on how you are using these potent words, "I am." What qualities or ways of being in the world make up your unique identity?

Now write down ten beliefs or maxims which you hold strongly. These should be your convictions, your values, or your morals that never change. Once you've written them, study them for awhile and see what they reveal about who you think you are. How are these beliefs related to the answers you gave to the question "Who are you?" Allow yourself to experiment in your mind with another set of beliefs. Are there any beliefs in your current list that you are ready to let go of? Who would you be if you held a different set of beliefs? Give yourself permission to expand, and see what you discover.

This question of identity is a serious issue, potentially ruling our entire life. Whatever we become identified with will dominate us, and whatever we can disidentify from, we can direct and use. Before we can ever become whole or healed, we must be clear about exactly who we believe we are and what we believe we are here for. Otherwise, life has no meaning. We'll live as egos, looking outward to others for our identities. We'll buy into each illusion that appeals to us at the moment—the ideal lover, the career that pays well financially, the perfect vacation. These limited goals miss the point of our incarnation story, which is a very "high" story indeed, rich with meaning and sacred purpose.

Our central core is a spark of the Divine. Most people, however, haven't consciously had a direct experience of God or of their own numinous inner nature. Though these sacred experiences are unfolding within our subjective lives on a regular basis, many will discount them as figments of the imagination. They do not yet realize their outer lives are only a reflection of a much greater Life, the archetypal process that "lives us" from our inner nature. To escape the trap of perpetually looking outward for our identity, we must use the bird's-eye view to bring our potential wholeness into focus. The wingless bird cannot see it.

The Self is *not* the ego! Make this distinction right now. The Self *dons* the ego so it can identify with society and relate to the status quo—so it can fit in well enough to do its sacred work. The ego is only your outer shell, the part of you that takes all the grief! Your ego is your soul's personality, the mask created so your soul can take on human form.

The egos of people who know nothing of the Self are defensive and fearful. When the ego is wounded, it behaves irrationally. It projects its emotionality onto others. Fear is very understandable since people who don't know the Self are not aware of their center.

Anytime we function, even for a moment, as a whole Self, we get a deep sense of well-being, sometimes even a peak experience. These unexplainable, non-ordinary events happen occasionally to many people. In fact, a poll indicated that over 70 percent of Americans claim to have had at least one mystical experience. We call these encounters with the Self "non-ordinary." Isn't this a shame? Why couldn't our identity as this real Self be our "ordinary" experience? Well, it can, and this book shows you how.

But I must warn you: Be sure that you are willing and sincere. In our work we say:

Let Reality govern my every thought, and Truth be the Heart of my life.

We've learned that this means that all untruth in our life falls away. Dying to our illusions is accompanied by sorrow and pain. But we also say good-bye to these unneeded parts of our identity with a certain sigh of relief; for our illusions, though they die hard, are quite troublesome to our evolving soul.

HOW THE SELF "WORKS US" AND TRANSFORMS OUR NATURE

Each individual ego is a crucible for the creation of consciousness and a vessel to serve as a carrier of that consciousness. The psyche is the Holy Grail, made holy by what it contains . . . Every human experience, to the extent that it is lived in awareness, augments the sum total of consciousness in the universe, [giving] each individual a role in the ongoing world-drama of creation.

—EDWARD EDINGER, *The Creation of Consciousness*

W hen we shift our focus to the God-within, we encounter archetypes and other subjective realities, for our inner nature is not physical, it is psychic and personal. We can access this inner world through imagery, impressions, flashes of inspiration, intuitive hints, memories, and other kinds of instantaneous direct knowing.

Our subjective life operates under a different set of rules than does the concrete, objective world. The inner Self is more an artist than a scientist; it makes itself understood through association and interpretation rather than through observation. Yet psychic events are facts. Though the events themselves cannot be measured by scientific means, their effects on our lives are observable and can be measured. For instance, a woman who relives her childhood sexual abuse so vividly that its painful energies are released and healed might lose easily the fifty pounds she has been carrying around for years as unconscious protection against being touched.

Archetypes arrange psychic energy into patterns we can discern. Like the organs in our physical body, archetypes function in our psyches to bring a pure quality to fruition or to dismantle an illusion that's blocking our growth. Archetypes personify our abstract Self and build mental images of our ideals. We must have an image of something in our minds before it can be created. This psychological law explains sayings like "thought is creative" and "energy follows thought."

Archetypal influences act on our subconscious in much the same way human instincts act on us biologically. Just as we react automatically by fight or flight when we encounter danger, so too we react automatically in psychodynamic ways. We may even feel these reactions in our bodies. For instance, if we've never integrated the archetype of Power, we may overreact psychically to even mild criticism by becoming excessively angry or defensive. When we are under the influence of archetypal energies, spontaneous reactions come upon us with fate-like inevitability.

However, when we focus consciously on a specific archetype, we activate it in our lives so that it can become a transformer. Some patterns in our life activate archetypal motifs—the perfect Lover, the ideal Warrior, an act of Courage, the classic Betrayal, and so on. Our processes can also be archetypal. Cycles of Death, Birth, and Transformation are experienced universally by every human, regardless of culture.

Other archetypes are key players in our divine unfolding, such as the Higher Mind, the Observer Self, the Heart—these are pure expressions of our divine essence. Higher Mind is the archetype we'll learn most about here. But you can make any one of them your guide whenever the situation calls for the special traits inherent in that archetype. The Self wears many faces in its archetypal dimension, just as the ego behaves as various people at different times.

It's important to remember that archetypes have archetypal nature only, not physical nature. These powers are available for anyone to tap into. To say I am the Messiah, or the Divine Feminine, would be egotistically to "hog the show." It could even be dangerous or psychotic. Rather, we absorb an archetype's characteristics and own and recognize its influence on our consciousness. We only know archetypes, in fact, by their powerful impulses and their imprints upon our lives.

Archetypal interplay is very active during certain cycles in our lives when transformation is necessary. The archetype's function is to bring on a powerful crisis of some kind—to focus us on a higher level of consciousness, in which everything is symbolic. They bring us a taste of our bigger story.

Once, during a week's meditation retreat, I saw Shiva dancing in the trees through the shadows and light of the leaves against the dark sky. I stayed up all night to partake in this amazing event. The next night I tried to make it happen again, but the magic was gone. Such precious moments are "visits from the gods." They cannot be counted on to be a regular part of our everyday reality.

Unfortunately, we're usually aware only of the more newsworthy events of our world, so we see more of archetypal negativity than we do of the grand acts of courage or reverence for life that humanity also brings forth. We must also keep these higher aspects of our nature in mind while we pass through humanity's "dark night."

The archetype of the Self observes us from on high and, when active, affects us on every level of consciousness, leaving no part of our old identity untouched. This is why we must learn to activate our Observer Self as a daily spiritual practice—so its archetypal function can enlighten us about all our actions and reactions. At the close of the millennium, each of us is making all of humanity's issues conscious. Our instinctual past and our archetypal future are at war within our psyches at times, attempting to make us whole. Our Observer Self will bring us closer to our completion.

The key to our freedom is for each of us to do our

part in this cocreative process and commit to heal ourselves and focus on the highest good. Here is the magic formula for success:

First, we must observe. Second, change our course to refocus on what we spiritually intend. These are the powers of Sincerity and Willingness in action. Then, the rest moves ahead on its own; the rest is Higher Power's "part."

Your real Self continually guides you through intuitive hunches, deep insights, or revelations—those "ahas!" that come from out of the blue that you know are inspired. The Self even creates the content of your dreams. If you have spontaneous dreams, with images, symbols, and meanings far beyond what your ego brain knows, you must realize some kind of Grand Designer is at work.

EXERCISE: REFLECTING ON ARCHETYPES IN YOUR LIFE

Take a moment now to reflect on a period in your life when you went through a powerful transformative experience—a time when you sensed that Destiny had a strong influence on your life . . . Once you recall this time, try to remember the quality or trait at the core of the experience. Recall the feelings that led up to this event . . .

What was really going on at the archetypal level during this intense time? Observe this from your Higher Mind. Let the image or idea behind the experience emerge . . . Once you capture this in your mind, you've discovered the archetypal process that was represented. This can lead you to see the larger pattern for this aspect of your individuation.

YOUR MIND IS A MAGICIAN

The words "I am" are potent words. Be careful what you hitch them to. The thing you're claiming has a way of reaching back and claiming you.

—A. L. KITSELMAN

So now you're becoming conscious of how to use your Higher Mind. Whatever the mind believes is real will eventually manifest itself. Often, it's the personal myths and story lines we've invented with our egos that have held us back. These are the "middle-sized stories" mythologist Joseph Campbell cautioned us to avoid creating. It's not that our limitations haven't really existed; they probably have. But the way we perceive them, hold on to them, and build them into dramas or lopsided views is usually at the root of our suffering. Our potential for using our minds to create myths that are life-giving is protection against these self-destructive habits.

Your Higher Mind is the principle, or archetype, around which all human thought is organized. It is the blueprint for perfect reason, for a holistic outlook in every situation—the bird's-eye view. Your Observer

Self is an expression of the Higher Power's Mind. It notices and reminds us that we've taken a wrong turn. Your Higher Mind observes every situation with the keen eye of pure reason. *But this observation is not an intellectual function. The Observer Self is a felt awareness—experienced as a "Moment of Truth."* It is those few seconds of direct inner knowing that come from out of the blue. It awakens you, then moves back and lets your conscious self decide what your next right action should be.

This is how the Observer Self transforms your life—through simple moment-by-moment action, teaching you gently to take responsibility for your life. Without it we could never evolve beyond the limitations of a wounded ego. This faithful inner helper guides you to a state of Self-realization.

The important thing to remember, though, is not to use this spiritual view to see how high you can be, but to see integration in it all. Wholeness encompasses both our light side and our darker side. Through aligning your little will with Divine Intelligence, you'll learn truly to accept everything that happens as having a sacred purpose for your life. Our personal will then becomes the "will-to-good," and we do no harm to others, for now we revere all life. Our Higher Mind is the unswerving arrow-like Will of God coming into form through us.

Acting alone, our ego can misdirect us toward addictive or dysfunctional ways of thinking, feeling, or behaving. We experience this when we are caught in an emotional reaction, motivated by unmet needs. These times of emotional imbalance cause us to run amuck, strengthening our delusions about power and control. People who abuse others emotionally are generally out of touch with their Observer Self.

If you are willing, stop a moment and reflect on a time when you've let an emotional reactivity or extreme bias run ahead of your intelligence, and you said or did something that was harmful to someone. The following guided imagery will help you reflect:

GUIDED IMAGERY: SEEING FROM THE BIRD'S-EYE VIEW

Find a quiet place to be still for a while, and put yourself into a meditative state. Close your eyes and breathe quietly for a few minutes, simply watching your breath move slowly in and out, saying to yourself "rising, falling, rising, falling" with each breath, until you feel serene. You can put on some calming, meditative music if this helps you go into a light trance.

Feel yourself leaving regular time and entering into a timeless state, a sacred place . . . Using your creative imagination, see yourself in your mind's eye involved in the particular condition you wish to release. See as vividly as you can a scene where this drama is playing out, and focus intently on it for several seconds, involving yourself completely in it . . . Feel the feelings that accompany this experience . . . all the way through . . . Really involve yourself! . . . (take a long pause)

And now, see yourself pulling up and out of this created scenario. Lift up, as though you are rising above it . . . (take a long pause) Once you are completely up and out, look back down at what you've left. See the scene unfolding through the eyes of your Observer Self. See your pain, your actions, your desires. See what is motivating you . . . (take a long pause)

See the "other" in the scene, and see that person's intentions and actions. See the whole situation all at once. Feel intuitively its nature and its purpose. And just allow this awareness to slowly penetrate your mind and heart . . . (take a long pause)

Send light and love to all who are in the scene. Feel this light and love penetrate everyone there until the whole thing dissolves in a flash of light . . . (take a long pause) Make this light and love become a felt experience; stay with this until this happens in your consciousness . . .

Now, just allow it all to dissolve . . . Feel it disappear as it slowly settles into your consciousness . . . When the energy has dissipated gradually, bring yourself back by slowly opening your eyes and becoming aware of your body, the room around you, and how you are feeling . . . (take a long pause)

Take some time to slowly integrate this experience. Reflect on your emotions when you were "down there" caught up in your predicament. Name these feelings. Then, recall how you felt when you were "up there," unattached to the detail and viewing it from a larger perspective. Now, name these feelings.

Upon completing this experiment, you may be surprised to note that it is the detached, impersonal Self who is the most loving—not the self who is so personally and intimately involved! Yet we've been trained to believe the opposite.

You may want to meditate, reflect, draw an image or symbol that came to you, or write in your journal for a while to make this experience fully conscious.

Be honest with yourself, and see if you can get hold of the pattern. What set you off? What need caused you to become so intense? What was your mind telling you that made you react in this manner? Herein will lie your attachment, the complex you may be trapped in. Where might you be stuck in your development? Reflect on all this for a while through the eyes of your Higher Mind.

On a higher, spiritual level, these same urges that compelled you to overreact emotionally are transmuted into compassion for others, and integrating them enables you to wield spiritual force with caution, love, and understanding. Try not to blame yourself if you've made emotional mistakes. For our transformation to occur, the fires of crisis must burn hot—that is why crises are life-altering experiences and pain is our greatest teacher.

The commitment to own our emotional wounds and one-sided views unites us with spiritual purpose. Our personal passions become compassionate service as we grow in maturity and learn to balance our intense emotions. We don't want to relinquish our passionate nature in favor of lukewarm living. This would make life very uninteresting. But, as one of my guides remarked, "May the earnestness of all those egos become the joy of our One Soul!"

You can probably recall a time when a dream image or symbol materialized in your outer life. Those chance occurrences, when a symbol and your outer life seem to have exactly the same meaning, are what we call synchronicity. Synchronicity appears most often when our lives are highly charged with a sense of destiny, when something archetypal is at work.

In our psychological life, we are always trying to reconcile some polarity, constantly needing to discriminate between right and wrong choices. We also know that we can be judgmental and fail to see the good in both sides of anything or anyone, denying the side we judge as negative.

Since we're programmed biologically and emotionally by a doubling process, duality resides at the core of our nature as human beings. Two-ness is actually a foundation block for our growth. We can learn to live within this tension of opposites, like a world-class surfer on a wave, cocreating an ever-possible new and higher self-concept that integrates both sides in a complementary fashion. From the winged bird's view where Oneness outshines duality, we can see that our consciousness is creative.

We have a powerful role in our evolution. Not all of it individually, of course. It takes all of us together to make up our world. But we are responsible for our part. Therefore, we must take seriously these three facts:

- Our thoughts are creative.

- We are life's one and only meaning-makers.

- Dualism is part of our design and must be acknowledged, worked through, and accepted before it can be transcended.

This means outer circumstances may not really be your problem or even need to change that much. But how you label all this content, assign it meaning, and interact with it creates what you call your life. Your Observer sees all your reactivity as your silent inner witness and reminds you, with no stake in the outcome, when you are becoming lost or out of balance because of some emotionally laden circumstance.

This fair witness consciousness shows you the whole scene through a broader lens. It gently points out what is really going on behind all this confusion. It helps us see the situation through the eyes of compassion. On an archetypal level, the Observer Self is our principle of Truth.

Western Nigerian medicine men called this power of Inner Truth the god Fa, who lives in the Beyond, the transcendent world beyond our ego-created reality. In their belief system, each of us has an invisible soul, or Life Principle. Anyone who wishes to know himself or herself while living this transitory life must go inward to connect with Fa, the only link to the Beyond. The Nigerian god Fa is what we have been calling the Observer Self, our connection to the Source who can reveal the true greatness of life.

Often, when we're having great difficulty letting go of an outworn or destructive pattern, the Observer will walk us through it one step at a time while we're wide awake and *acutely* aware of what we're doing. The Self will give us a vignette in vivid color, so we can see our pattern mirrored back. This process can be very uncomfortable, but it is often necessary for our healing. When we can get a breath of fresh thought in between all of our actions and reactions, we can change our behavior on the spot.

Sometimes, we can even see our predicament with humor. This means a healing is in progress; we're getting unattached. You might have an insight like, "Gradually now, some balance is restored so I can get over my reactivity and face the reality before me. Then, I'll see that a great lesson is being enacted, just for my benefit." Once we've seen something consciously, we can never be unconscious of it again. We may choose to (and sometimes do) *feign* unconsciousness, but now we'll know better. What an ingenious, loving Knower we have built right into us!

Once we uncover our major patterns and integrate any loose ends still holding us prisoners of fear, judgment, doubt, or misunderstanding, we are free. And we begin to live in the present with the joy of being fully awake and consciously participating in our own creation story as a felt experience.

WE'RE ALL PLAYERS IN THE DIVINE WORLD DRAMA—BUT WHO'S THE PLAYWRIGHT?

If one knows that one has been singled out by divine choice and intention from the beginning of the world, then one feels lifted beyond the transitoriness and meaninglessness of ordinary human existence, and transported to a new state of dignity and importance, like one who has a part in the divine world drama.

—CARL JUNG, *Psychology and Religion: West and East*

L ike a staged play, your life is being acted out while you learn to be loving and true to your highest nature. You may not realize it, but we all create story lines based on how we see ourselves and how we interpret each experience. Once we create our story, we live it out as though it were the Truth. Every participator in our drama then plays out a role exactly as we've defined it. This reality picture is what you are creating from that big world of possibilities. Watch your own life and see!

When we become trapped in some old, limited shoreline that not longer serves us, we begin to suffocate and so do our relationships. We can get so entangled in our plots, we forget our greater purpose. When we can feel our connection to our Source, we are sustained, even in our darkest hours.

Your role, then, in this divine world scheme is to be willing to step out and be fully your Self. We humans are the only species in all the kingdoms of nature who can make meaning and who can feel compassion for the whole.

Our consciousness, as you can now see, works like a searchlight. We sense something in the spiritual world, feel inspired, and bring it to this world, giving it a name. It can be an idea, a product, a relationship, a dream, a talent, a hope—whatever. We are materializing spirit. Conversely, we can see something in this world through our spiritual perspective. When we do this, we are spiritualizing matter. In other words, when we can give something in our mundane lives significant meaning or sacred purpose, we have spiritualized it. *This is how we spiritualize the material world—step by step, event by event.*

While we are living this way, we begin to grow more enlightened. As we begin to see the Higher Self in others, we spiritualize *them*. And they do the same for us. We all learn to acknowledge and empower one another for our true talents, visions, and dreams. We start to shine, and as we become more comfortable with ourselves, we encourage others to shine as well.

Though we learn to become more connected to others, we are constantly guided from within by the inner Knower. We let more and more of our true selves show. Whenever we slip below this level of consciousness and function automatically or in our old ways, our Observer prompts us.

Later on, when we are all more enlightened, we'll begin to materialize as Spirit; we'll walk this earth as one who lives from the viewpoint of the winged bird. We'll be following the path of the Christ, the Buddha, or whoever models authenticity for us. We will be part of implementing a divine plan as courageous cocreators.

To consciously choose to become a fully realized being means you are volunteering to be used by the forces of evolution. Instead of just letting nature take its course, individuating you gradually, you will enter onto an accelerated path. And you will transform by leaps and bounds through rapid sequences of death and rebirth. Does this sound familiar? Stop and think for a minute about your own growth pattern over the past few years.

EXERCISE: TAKING STOCK OF YOUR LIFE

Now, stop a minute and quickly take stock of your life. Think about the qualities of your current relationships and circumstances. How are you seen by your intimates concerning

• your mental equanimity?

- your emotional maturity?
- your need to be in control?

What is the quality of your primary relationship? It is here, within the domain of intimacy, that we most often are shown our deepest wounds and our most imbedded attachments or addictions. Be honest. No one is listening but you. Perhaps your Higher Mind has an objective comment to make on your behalf at this point.

If you have a major issue still leftover, floating around unhealed, you may need to take some time out, find a therapist or spiritual guide, and go deeply into yourself for a while. Your time of completion may have come. Your identity may be ready to expand beyond what you've always thought you were.

THE DIVINE LAW OF
REDEMPTION

The fates lead him who will; those who won't they drag.

—ROMAN SAYING

Concepts like redemption and salvation were never intended to be interpreted morally. These are "psychic functions," meaning they interact with your subjective psychological life to produce a *felt* change. To *redeem* something means to go back, take another look, and heal a situation through the eyes of understanding. Redemption is not about being good or bad; it's about realigning ourselves with our true intention whenever we've gotten off the mark.

When we are undergoing a transformation, we will encounter the workings of the Divine Law of Redemption. We will have the urge to complete any unfinished business or unresolved issues within our personal subconscious, any wounds left over from times we have repressed or denied our real feelings or true nature. Your Observer Self will pick up on this compelling urge. It will make you aware whenever one of your issues surfaces; it will guide you to the help you need.

Redemption is accomplished by recognizing and integrating your unconscious aspects. But healing is a process, not an event; so it will not happen overnight. Therefore, the first part of your process is to *descend* back through your past. The Law of Redemption takes us back through memory lane to retrieve lost and valuable pieces of our lives.

Combining the winged bird's vantage point and your sense of compassion, you'll be able to look back and feel what it is you must release, or retrieve and integrate. This process is true and practical spiritual work. From your transcendent point of view you'll note that you've been trapped in some illusion. Maybe you have been hooked by an unmet need. This is a time to check out every motive, especially those related to things in your life that are taking a lot of your energy or time.

Without the Higher Mind that remains holistic and keeps an archetypal perspective, you can get trapped in your limited human viewpoint. To free us from this trap, shamans do soul retrieval work, and spiritual psychologists work with the process of redemption.

This process of redeeming our wounded or unintegrated fragments enables us to establish in Truth that which could have been lost through misinterpretation. Truth is that tiny mustard seed within every experience that is planted in our consciousness and grows into something substantial, some quality we carry forward from each experience that is real and useful for humanity.

For example, perhaps you are a social worker specializing in child abuse. You become highly esteemed in your community You even receive a public award. What happens if the job ends, if you are forgotten, if the medal rusts? The form side of experience fades. What lives on is the essence, the quality of the courage, compassion, or service you gave, not only from doing a good job, but also from facing your own unresolved issues placed in front of you daily as you worked with clients. You were changed. And your soul can now use these qualities for the sake of the whole.

HEALING THE HUMAN SHADOW

The purpose of the shadow is to provide the human soul with the opposition and tension to develop tough inner resolve and determination to clarify through the tension of the opposites.

—JOHN CONGER, *The Body as Shadow*

Your Observer Self is the tamer of your shadow side, the dark, unloved, unlived part of your nature. Your shadow is a conglomeration of the traits you deplore and prefer to notice in others but never, of course, in yourself. It consists of parts of your psyche that were damaged or didn't mature and of which you are ashamed. You have disowned these parts of yourself. Your psyche has built up defense mechanisms to keep you away from knowing these aspects of your nature.

But this doesn't mean these traits disappear. When denied, they grow stronger—buried in closets of repression in your subconscious mind. This shadowy side of your nature—usually a form of aggressiveness, meanness, hysteria, or forbidden sexual fascination—hides out just below the surface of your awareness. It acts out when you are off-guard—when you have not eaten or slept enough, or when stress is making you feel frustrated or helpless. On these occasions it may burst out in an out-of-control overreaction and embarrass you. The more it is denied, the stronger its force. As though in a pressure cooker, your shadow chums with all those pent-up feelings you're denying or are too ashamed to explore in the light of day.

But to be rounded out, we must make our shadow and all the fear and rejection associated with it conscious, or we'll be at its mercy forever. To heal, the shadow has to be exposed and accepted for exactly who and what it is. Then, paradoxically, it won't need to act out so dramatically, though it may still tug at you from time to time. It will always be your dark side.

Your shadow is only the *antithesis* side of the creative process—the "sparring partner" who makes your life exciting. It forces you to weed out anything wrong with your design and to look at what you're trying to ignore. Its sacred function is to force you to work through your dark side, so its energy can be released in appropriate ways. Then, it blesses you with its spiritual gift: it releases your *élan vital*. Your shadow represents some of your passions that have been ill-placed or possibly repressed completely.

Coming to terms with the shadow is very much like managing and loving a hyperactive child. We learn to express our true feelings in safe settings, see them operate, forgive ourselves and others, and learn to accept it all, over and over . . . until all our energies are balanced and can be used for good. This is integration.

When you feel yourself moving toward an overreaction, call on your Observer Self to watch you consciously. You can either do this symbolically in your mind, or you can act it out in the outer world. But be careful about the choice of acting out your shadow; doing so can cause you more problems. If you just can't stop yourself from acting out, then you need a lesson.

In shadow work, we can learn to have an ongoing dialogue with the differing voices of the shadow, along with all the taunting images that challenge us when we're trying to stop a destructive habit. By clarifying our images and our energies, we will eventually integrate our shadow self enough so it will no longer threaten us.

At times you may need an objective other such as a therapist or a friend who can help you. It's pretty difficult to see beyond yourself. It is impossible, as the saying goes, to "pull ourselves out of the swamp by our own pigtail."

One night as I was dozing in that place between waking and sleep, my Observer Self kicked in and said, "Look. A very old friend is here for a visit." Then I saw someone with my inner eye who looked very familiar. She was decked out as a classic Southern belle—billowy hat, flowing ribbons, and all. And very inappropriately, she was out in the middle of a lake all by herself trying to row a boat, standing up and wobbling all around in the choppy water. I wanted to smile and cry at the same time. I could see so plainly her vulnerability and helplessness—ludicrous for one so bright. I realized she was an aspect of myself I'd been living with for as long as I could remember. My heart melted, and I wanted to reach out to her.

I heard myself say, "Well, hello there, dear little Sally. I recognize you. You've lived in me, my mom, and all my aunts. I see you with all your funny, coquettish ways. And I think I love you—because quite frankly, I admire your spunk!" In my dream, I saw the two of us merge. I took off that silly hat, rolled up my sleeves, sat down in the boat, and rowed to the other shore.

My shadow has become my friend. I know her now as the undeveloped, shadowy side of my nature. Consciousness is light; it is the energy of Love. Something is about to show itself so it can be faced, and thereby healed.

HITTING BOTTOM IS A
SACRED FUNCTION

In such a period of change and growth, emergence is often experienced as emergency, with all its attendant stress.

—ROLLO MAY, *The Courage to Create*

H itting bottom is a stage on the journey we all must face. We reach this point in almost every transformational cycle. Let's dismantle the illusions around this theme, which is so dreaded and feared. Hitting bottom is the shift we make from being involved in a condition to evolving back out of it. The process of identification and disidentification contains a turning point:

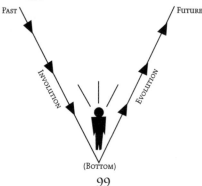

PAST

FUTURE

INVOLUTION

EVOLUTION

(BOTTOM)

99

Though hitting bottom feels awful, it has a sacred purpose which can be seen from "above the storm." At bottom, you no longer have the psychological defenses that keep you from your deepest Truth. So there you sit, with exactly what is. Like Humpty-Dumpty, nothing can put you together again. Your old identity is gone. This is a time for you to be fully yourself. You need time to regain your perspective.

We must all pass through times like this, when something comes to an end, and we haven't a clue what's coming next. When these times hit, we need to grieve our losses. We must take some time to die to everything as we knew it. Sometimes we may sit in our misery for quite a while before our next right step comes into view.

In our work, we call this condition "hanging in the dangle." We all hate this stage. Even our keen, observing Higher Mind seems to vanish at times like this; we can't seem to find the bigger picture. We must accept our helplessness and ambiguity for now, feeling pulled this way and that, crying our tears, wailing out our rage. We must deal honestly with whatever feelings we have—until the cosmic clock comes round and brings us new life. Rebirth is always just around the corner from the bottom.

Anytime you start getting hooked back into an old pattern, you need to return to your higher identity, the Self at the top. You may go back and forth for a while, like a pendulum swinging between attachment and nonattachment, between your old and your wobbly new identity. Sometimes it feels like you're regressing instead of moving forward. This isn't an easy time for anyone. It's time to disidentify and move on to your next destination.

Let go, look to your Higher Self for help, and your evolution will guide you up and out. From the bottom, your Higher Mind will show you a glimpse of the bigger picture. You'll find something to believe in again, and once more, life will seem worthwhile. Some new ideal, some new goal will take shape. Soon, new people will start coming into your life. And off you can go toward another dream.

THE DAILY PRACTICE
OF SELF-REMEMBRANCE

The ego is a marvelous fiction . . . .(It) is a novel writ-
ten by ourselves about ourselves, and the very first step
on the Quest is to disentangle ourselves from its seduc-
tions and to dis-identify with the manuscript we, and
the collective consensus around us, have managed to
create.

—YATRI, *Unknown Man, the Mysterious Birth of a New Species*

Now that you're waking up, the process of Self-remembrance will become a way of life. Recognized and invited, the observing, nonattached Higher Mind will move into the forefront of your thoughts when you are "asleep at the wheel" and about to make some grave mistake. The Observer Self will refocus your attention back to the Truth of any situation.

Here is an example: You're in the midst of repri-manding your teenage daughter, righteously uphold-ing a long-established family rule. You may be border-ing on emotional abuse as your voice rises and you begin to pontificate. Suddenly, the Observer nudges you: "Remember, your daughter is individuating—looking for a reason to leave home. Something larger is at stake here." And instantly, through this deeper awareness, you are brought out of your robot-like over-reaction long enough to take a breath and see the whole picture. Your mother pushed the same emotional buttons in you; now, as though on automatic, you are treating your daughter the same way. What nonsense, you realize. Yesterday's "grit" has clouded your view.

Now awake, you speak to your daughter more gently from your heart. You still tell her your truth, but without the pompous intensity in your voice. Heart to heart, we can always hear one another.

Here is a simple practice you can use when you need to bring your Observer Self into the picture:

EXERCISE: AWARENESS TRAINING

Begin by saying, "I am aware . . . " at least three times a day, preferably in the morning. Then make a genuine attempt to observe consciously everything you do and are—your activities, thoughts, feelings, needs. At first, you may come to awareness only a few times during the day, and then only for a minute or two. But don't be discouraged. This practice is quite humbling at first, for you will see just how asleep you generally are!

You might wish to stop reading and practice being aware for a few minutes. First, note what your body is doing right now . . . Then your emotions . . . How are you feeling in your gut? Now, take a minute to watch your thoughts and observe the workings of your brain . . . You'll get to a place where you'll see that you're not your body, you're not your feelings, nor are you the contents of your mind. You are that Higher One who watches it all.

Here's another practice that can help you clear the static that might interfere in the communication between you and your Observer Self:

EXERCISE: OBSERVING YOUR INNER CRITIC

Sometimes when you are trying to listen for the clear advice of your Observer Self, another voice in your head will interfere, criticizing or shaming you for the error you just made. Your ego's inner critic has intruded. You will recognize this voice by its intensity and harsh tone. It is invested in an outcome, whereas the Observer never is.

When this happens, go higher and observe that you're in a reactive state. Ask yourself what grit from your past is getting in the way of your present awareness. The inner critic speaks with the voice of your wounded ego in need of healing. Try to discover why this voice is in your head now.

Is it serving some function? If so, try to understand its message. If it's not serving a function, recognize that the inner critic is just an old habit you're ready to release.

When you get used to seeing situations from the Higher Mind's wider spectrum, you'll begin to see clearly how some processes and people hook you, while other situations just seem to flow on by.

When a current situation or a person reminds you of an old hurt, something you've not made conscious, an unhealed complex may be activated. For example, if you have not fully individuated from your mother, any situation that reminds you of your habitual pattern of interactions with her may activate your "mother complex." Because you are still caught up in the past, your mother's feelings become yours. If she disapproves of you, you disapprove of you! Observing consciously shakes loose these patterns so they can heal.

Here's a quick imagery exercise that will help you disengage from unhealed authority issues:

EXERCISE: GETTING HOOKED AND UNHOOKED

First analyze the situation and ask for clarity about what is really going on. What is activated when you are feeling reactive? What did the situation call for? What was it they said? When exactly did your feelings start becoming intense? Is this a familiar feeling? What is the common denominator in situations like this? What is it that is making a scene like this part of your reality? The answers to these questions will show you what is required to become centered in your Self.

Now see an inner image of your mother (or father, or any authority figure) . . . Notice her stance, the quality of energy she carries, how she habitually behaves . . . (pause) Now picture yourself stepping away from this image . . . And now you are standing free . . . Take a moment to breathe in this new you! Really let yourself feel the separation. And know that it is real . . . (long pause)

Use your imagination to see this separation happening . . . Do this over and over, as many times as you need to, until the inner image becomes clear, and you experience yourself as an individual standing apart from the other.

Watch how you behave when you are really free of this old pattern.

Another unskillful behavior pattern that may at times block the clear voice of your Higher Self is holding on to anger. Staying angry at someone who has hurt you takes a lot of energy. You have to shut down other, more positive parts of yourself in order to stay focused on old resentments. It's best to release them—for your own mental health.

"But," you say, "this person really did abuse me. She does not deserve to be forgiven. She has been genuinely unkind." This way of thinking contains an error: Forgiving people does not release them from their own karmic debts. Karmic forgiveness is between the person who has done wrong and the divine balance of the universe. Rather, forgiving another is important to free up your own energy, which is designed for greater things. Your forgiveness is *for you.*

Once you know who you are, everyone is seen for who they are and appreciated for their part in this divine world drama, mistakes and all. Sometimes our enemies are our greatest teachers.

Any time you are feeling something from its highest, most sacred point in consciousness while simultaneously knowing the meaning of it, you are engaging what we call "Transpersonal Viewing." For that moment, you are enraptured. You've stepped into the Beyond, the place Jung called the *unus mundus* ("one world") behind all apparent worlds. Such intensely felt archetypal experiences bring us total fulfillment. For that moment, we are whole.

Your Higher Mind will eventually bring you a direct experience of the Divine that will show you without a doubt that you are more than what you have always thought you were—and that there is, indeed, a greater world.

When Jung was asked whether he believed in God, he replied, "No, I don't *believe* in God; I *know* God." Transpersonal Viewing will give you this same certainty. Powerful transpersonal experiences not only gratify our deepest longing, they heal the psyche. Once we befriend our Higher Mind, these experiences will happen often. When we've faced it all, owned it all, and let go of our illusions about how things ought to be, we can relax and enjoy the ride.

Once your Observer Self becomes your constant conscious companion, you'll be aware that your self-image is changing and expanding. You'll see that *how* you observe a thing determines the what of it. Modern physicists know this now, having finally caught up with what the mystics of every age have always known:

> *We are never born and we never die;*
> *for we are consciousness itself.*

YOUR BIGGER STORY

Without the transcendent and the transpersonal, we get sick . . . or else hopeless and apathetic. We need something bigger than we are to be awed by and to commit ourselves to.

—ABRAHAM MASLOW

I n your Higher Mind, your personal story is spread out over a much longer time line than your ordinary biography. Remember, you have archetypal significance, too! Let's go higher now and view you from a wider lens, from the World of Meaning. The memories of humanity's One Soul are stored in this higher world.

If you're willing, take a few deep breaths, and let your consciousness move into a timeless, sacred space. And then, listen:

You came into a preselected family for the sacred purpose of incarnation to heal this particular part of humanity. You inherit traits and weaknesses of your predecessors, then make them conscious to heal or learn from them whatever your soul intends. Your genes are encoded with certain strengths, talents, and distortions that are to be released, expressed, erased, integrated, or transformed. You do this by taking on all that you inherited and then becoming conscious of it. You make spiritually based choices that resolve or correct the problems you carry and represent. Humanity can only be healed by your *assimilation* and *transmutation* of the human condition itself.

In this incarnation you are here to heal this world and help it evolve to its next level. *This is your sacred purpose for being on this planet.* You are the rescue mission! This is the function of our species. This is our part and it has always been so. No one can do this task for us.

The first part of your life, then, was lived for the sake of your ego's development and its adjustment to the culture in which you were born. Your ego lives on the surface; it is the face consciousness wears when it looks out at the world it is to inhabit. In psychology, the ego is referred to as the *persona*, which in Greek means "mask." The ego is our executor who figures out how to live in the outer world by watching others and mimicking society's current ideals. It picks up its cues from society's reward system. Remember when you were small? You wanted to be a good little boy or girl so you could have the ice-cream cone.

From the time we are born, we are being initiated into an outer reality, a culture that demands certain values and standards. So at first, by cosmic law, we are naturally preoccupied with getting our own needs met and with learning to form relationships and activities that will bring us growth.

This first stage of your awakening as a little human being may have been quite an ordeal, however. Flaws are built in right from the start. None of us had completely enlightened parents! This is simply a fact of life. Nor have we been all that wise in parenting our own children—or ourselves, for that matter. Inside your head live two voices, the voice of your ego and the voice of your Higher Self.

You must learn to discriminate between these voices. This daily practice your Observer Self performs requires a lot of inner work from you. The conflicts that arise from being unaware of the difference between the voices produce crises, which are your life's lessons. The word *crisis* is from the Greek word *krinein*, which means "to discriminate or decide." The Chinese word for crisis means "dangerous opportunity." A crisis will burn hot enough to open us up completely. Then, we can see from our larger reality.

You were born enlightened. You've always been aware of your true origins. But once you were physically embodied, you forgot. It isn't possible to remember our cosmic roots for long, and this forgetting is for a cosmic reason: We had to go into an unconscious state to take on fully our human conditions.

Sometimes very small children will shock you with their uncanny understanding of who they really are. I'm reminded here of a precious story I recently heard:

A four-year-old girl greeted her new baby brother

when he came home from the hospital and ordered her parents to leave the room while she spoke to him alone. The parents had some anxiety about this, because young children often resent newborns and want to harm them. So the parents ignored this suggestion, at which their daughter stomped her foot and demanded they leave! They stepped outside the door, keeping watch, and saw her bend over the crib and say to the baby, "Well, John, I'm glad you're finally here. And listen! You must tell me quickly before you forget: What is God like? I must know, 'cause I've nearly forgotten!"

The rules here were divined by our Higher Power and were modeled by the Christ, the Buddha, Lord Shiva, Shakti, and other Divine Beings who have come here as our enlightened Masters. Here is the dominant rule they each lovingly modeled for us:

> *We are to take it all on fully. And dance our way through life's experiences, both the joys and all the sorrows. And then, and only then, can we disidentify and rise on "up and out."*

It is written in your "job description" that at some point you must have the courage to come out and be your Self as our great teachers have done. No more copouts, no more games. No more superficial living. No more hiding from each other or from ourselves. This world is starving for authenticity, and you are it!

You model this awakening by simply evidencing the *faith* you have in the process, based on your own experience. You are a vision carrier, a light bearer for this world. This simple fact is all there is to it. Yours is such a simple task, yet so very removed from how we've all been programmed.

If you are like me, leaping and bounding through constant change, you probably could use a little supportive companionship along the way. Self-understanding provides a great cushion for this process. The company of others of like mind and intention is often our salvation. Here, in the fast lane, your world is rarefied. Many people get stuck along the way in the ego's world of outer focus, and it gets lonely! It's important to stay close to those who are awakening with you.

Once you commit to this way of living, you are in for a thrilling surprise: Your real kin will start to surface all around you when your awareness of the greater life is soundly established. When you meet one with whom you have a deep soul connection, you feel an instant recognition. You will share the quiet knowing that you truly understand each other—a deep, abiding, nonattached love.

These are your soul brothers and sisters, here to be involved in your true destiny. These are very ancient ties, yet newly discovered—like the return of a future memory. Through these deep connections, your life will become empowered with Spirit.

Like the pieces in a cosmic puzzle, we will each eventually find our correct fit. Then, we'll be in Right

Relationship. Ego and essence (soul), mind and heart, masculine and feminine, God and humanity, brother and sister, will have all become One.

So let's stop a minute now and remember why we came to this planet. Ask yourself, what is your true spiritual intention? What is the purpose of your life? If you knew for certain that you were going to die tomorrow, would you be able to say you have fulfilled your purpose here?

We all know we have wounds and shadows that must be dealt with and healed. In order to live out our spiritual intention fully and fulfill our sacred purpose, we must be willing to turn away from our past and toward our future, which is always emerging at the periphery of our conscious awareness.

The following guided imagery will enhance this inner work. Whenever you feel trapped in a pattern that no longer works for you and you truly seek release, this meditation will help you let it go. Be sure that you are ready, for this process invokes the archetype of Release or Dissolution, and any condition or relationship that is no longer furthering your growth will begin to dissolve.

GUIDED IMAGERY: RELEASING AN EMOTIONAL ATTACHMENT

First, say out loud, "I am willing to see this

116

pattern in its entirety and to accept it for what it is. I will no longer allow it to rule me."

Now say, "From this point forward, I am willing to become respondable to my Self. I am willing to recognize assistance when it comes and to do my part!"

Now, visualize yourself sitting in repose in the center of your Heart . . . and allow the pattern you wish to release to arise in your conscious awareness . . . Let it take you over . . . Feel this state of limitation or negativity as intensely as you can . . . (pause)

Rise above your vision of pattern, moving higher and higher. Experience how you gradually feel free as you move higher and higher . . . From above, see the whole pattern from a distance. See it for what it is . . . (pause)

Watch the pattern turn into a symbol representing its qualities . . . And give it a name! As you observe this symbol, notice that it is not you. Realize that you are the One observing, the One above.

Now, toss this symbol into the fire you see before you! . . . And watch it turn to flame and then gradually disintegrate into a powdery white ash . . . Stay with this image until the symbol of your problem or pattern is completely "whitened" and note how you feel as it dissolves . . . (long pause)

Take some time to say good-bye, and bless this pattern for serving you as it did . . . See the sacred function it had in your life . . . And feel as much gratitude as you can muster for what this pattern has represented for your growth . . .

Now, catch a quick glimpse of yourself behaving in the world free of this pattern you've just released . . . (pause) And anchor this new image in your mind . . . (long pause)

Sit in reverent silence for a few minutes and commune quietly with your Higher Self. Stay very close to the feelings emanating from your Heart . . . (long pause in the silence)

If any insights or instructions occur to you during this silent time, write them down as soon as possible. Meditation is like dreamwork; sometimes the revelations float by rapidly, and we do not catch them. Even if what is being revealed does not make sense right now, note it anyway.

Once you feel completed, return to your ordinary business in your usual ways—and await your next right step. You will know when it arrives.

In Divine Love there is no carpet to sweep anything under. Everything is seen, felt, and acknowledged. Each of us must take full responsibility. No one can do our part for us. Our problems are not just personal; neither is our healing or creative expression only for ourselves: Anytime we heal a condition in our personal lives or create some new and inspired response, a little more light shines brightly on our one humanity. . . A little more of real Self stands revealed.

Without the aid of the bird's-eye view, we would be lost in the maze of human fragmentation. With deep gratitude we can honor our inner Knower, our Higher Mind, for giving us the view that can contain all of who we are. This archetypal Self will always remind us of both our human frailties and our immortal divinity.

We can learn to be "above the storm," as Higher Mind, and know that all our experiences, even the painful ones, have a sacred purpose. And we can lovingly, even joyously, accept our plight. We forgive ourselves and one another for the mistaken notions and wrong turns we've made that became our instruments for transformation. From the silence of our one Heart, we can understand what the great Indian sage, Sri Aurobindo, meant when he told his disciple,

By thy stumblings, the world is perfected.

PART THREE

CREATING PURPOSE FOR OUR SPIRITUAL FUTURE

Where there is no vision, the people perish.
—PROVERBS 24:18

PRACTICAL MYSTICS ARISING!

There are two kinds of people . . . One kind you can just tell by looking at them at what point they congealed into their final selves. It might be a very nice self, but you know you can expect no more surprises from it. Whereas, the other kind keep moving, changing . . . They are fluid . . . moving forward . . . making new trysts with life, and the motion of it keeps them young. In my opinion, they are the only people who are still alive. You must be constantly on your guard, Justin, against congealing.

—GAIL GODWIN, *The Finishing School*

When an old world dies and the future opens, fiery souls with open minds and hearts aflame with purpose will carry us through. If this message inspires you, you must be one of those remarkable souls who is willing to make new trysts with life, who refuses to "congeal." Your love for humankind has the potent transcendental quality of magical *élan vital*—the essential ingredient for any new creation.

Today, because science and mysticism are merging, practical mystics are coming forward from within our own psyches, a new archetype emerging for today's transitional times. As the synthesis of the Seer and the Scientist, practical mystics know how to manifest the visionary in physical reality. These new helpers of humanity are not dreamers; they are doers of Spirit's work. They are free thinkers—and must be—in order to break away from the past and serve an evolving humanity.

The mystics of old spun visions of possible futures out of their hopes, wishes, and desires. They were knowers who could predict what was to come, not builders who could construct it. Today's new imaginative visionaries do not stop with an image of the ideal. They embody their dreams and build scaffolds through which Spirit can shine its light.

"God geometrizes," said the sage Pythagoras, the father of music and mathematics. Today's new seers move into the world of materialism with a steady eye, grounding humanity's visions in new institutions, systems, policies, and procedures that reshape our everyday world.

Practical mystics are never zealots. They know how to balance the tension of opposites and not get caught in one-sided emotionalism, at least never for very long. Their "Aquarian" consciousness respectfully carries forward the goods of the past, honoring all paths that represent true spirituality as approaches that lead one home.

But I must warn you: Those who are invested in upholding the status quo often regard today's mystics as complete fools. No matter. Possessed with a gutsy fortitude to buck society's stereotypes, the practical mystics of today remain obedient and courageous servants of Spirit, undaunted by any resistance they encounter in the outer world. Then, with an uncanny childlike grace, they inspire all of humanity to build its dreams.

In this final section of this book, you will be guided in techniques that will help you weave your way through the ordeals we must each encounter during any transformation. Most important, you will learn to hear more clearly the inner voice of your soul, so you can resonate to its messages and recognize this true authority who speaks to you from within.

Our subjective life is a rich storehouse of tools and techniques for unfolding our future. If focused upon with a positive intent, the images and symbols of humanity's collective unconscious coded into our psyches can help us journey through a maturation process that eventuates in our knowing what we came here to do and to be. The expanded human blueprint we then discover is based in Intelligence itself, the originator and divine completer of all our life experiences. Accessing this pattern of inner wholeness—even for a moment—puts us in touch with our true life's work.

When we experience the awesome numinosity of having something extraordinary express itself in our ordinary life, we are for that moment transfixed. We experience wholeness. The objective and subjective realities, which are our personal and divine selves, have merged. This marriage of the ego and the soul lays the foundation for a future Self to stand upon. As it is written in the Gospel according to St. Thomas:

> And Jesus said to them: When you make the two one, and when you make the inner as the outer, and the outer as the inner, and the above as the below . . . then you shall enter the Kingdom.

When the fire of your mystical soul ignites through the power of invocation, you feel a strong motivation to build that new "temple of humanity" that will house your incoming Self. You become fascinated with society's need for new forms and want to serve. To that end, you spontaneously begin to create a new vital body that coalesces around a new way of experiencing your Self. In other words, as you access a new archetypal potential, you step up a rung on the evolutionary ladder and become yourself the new creation you envision.

This unrelenting drive toward completion is the force of evolution itself. By becoming aware of the divine idea of who we'd like to be and taking the steps necessary to actualize this ideal, we create purpose which floods our present with our spiritual future.

BIRTHING A
NEW CONSCIOUSNESS

*The seeds of future events are carried within ourselves
They are implicit in us and unfold according to the
law of their own nature.*

— LAWRENCE DURRELL, *The Alexandria Quartet: Cleo*

Our past is but a foreshadowing of our future. Nothing that happens to us is irreversible, and no transformation is a final determination. We are always moving and changing, for this is our nature. This purpose-filled existence of ours, though timeless in intent, evolves dynamically along the chain of unfolding we call "time." We might even say that, as an evolving consciousness, *we are the journey itself!*

Birthing a new consciousness is accomplished by staying focused on our spiritual purpose—on why we incarnated on earth at this particular time. By such perpetual Self-remembrance, we continually draw the future into our present life. Spiritual purpose grounds us like a lightening rod while our "little story" rocks on, in positive or negative directions.

Identification, disidentification—this is how we move through time. We identify with whatever we need to know in our small stories, take it on and learn from it by becoming involved in it. Then, once we have learned what we need, we disidentify and move on. We were never intended to remain stuck in any one place in consciousness, or in any one event.

When we hold this sacred and purposeful attitude, we can readily see that nothing happens to us by accident. We see the meaning in small events, while our bigger story becomes our true reality. How good are you at taking on and becoming involved? And, even more important, how good are you at letting go? These are the questions we all need to ask ourselves.

ARCHETYPAL BLUEPRINTS SCULPT OUR FUTURE

Because we can picture them and comprehend their traits, archetypes are the symbolic mediators through which the divine plan materializes in time. Each of us represents certain archetypal patterns already, either consciously or unconsciously. As we learn to understand these patterns more deeply, we can discriminate better between the archetypes we wish to take on and those to which we should give no energy.

But archetypes are not just a personal matter. These symbolic patterns are carving out the future of humanity as well, operating in larger incarnational cycles than those of which we are generally aware.

When a great cycle ends and a new one must be put

into place, the door to the archetypal dimension stands wide open. Powerful forces of change put in place by the Creator are most active now, functioning in ways beyond our intellect's comprehension. This is why we often feel we've been dealt a blow by fate or had a miracle drop into our lives.

Our limited human ego struggles in vain against such powerful evolutionary forces. However, our archetypal Self, the nucleus of our greater design, resurfaces from within to guide us forward. This core Self, our embodied soul, is the promise of the future lying hidden within our ordinary existence.

We're being called now to put on an archetypal face that the Self can wear to befit the coming times. We are unsure how to do it, or what exactly to expect. But we feel its urges as our yearnings; we get glimpses and hints.

Remember, nothing we do is ever "just personal." Our willingness to stand tall, to embody the archetypes of evolutionary transformation—World Server, Warrior, Magician, Wise Woman, Hero, Healer—is vital to others who are traveling along with us. When we take on such archetypal identities, dressed in modern-day clothes, they interpenetrate our consciousness so they can act through us.

LIVING WITHIN THE TENSION OF THE OPPOSITES

Birthing a new consciousness is never an easy task. We've all got attachments and illusions we didn't even know we had until they start to unravel at the edges of our cherished identities and familiar comfort zones. There is no path until we step onto it; we must create it as we go.

We are always dying to the old while the new comes into formation. Quite naturally, this process creates a tension between who we've been and who we are becoming. The question is: Do we focus obsessively on where we have been and what we feel we're losing, or do we focus on what is becoming?

In the dimension of the Source, all opposites are present without conflict. But for us, contraries rub and jostle terribly. This tension of opposites generates tremendous psychic energy. We can either try to walk around the contradictions we experience, or we can progress through them. Dancing in the tension of opposites restructures us. As the mystical poet William Blake wrote in *Heaven and Hell*, "Without contraries there is no progression."

Sometimes the conflict we feel is between two aspects of our own nature. Other times the tension is between ourselves and the outer world, perhaps manifesting in a conflict with another person. Any kind of conflict can stir the seas of transformational chaos, releasing an energy we can work with. This "fire by friction" can stir the psyche strongly enough to open its storehouse of archetypal patterns to bring to birth the "third and higher thing" that resolves the oppositional conflict between the original two.

Too often we fail to take advantage of the opportunity for growth that inner conflicts give us. We fall prey to negative judgment of part of ourselves and to the tendency to repress "undesirable" parts of our nature. But our continued evolution—perhaps even our very survival—depends upon our owning this unredeemed shadow of ours and learning to live within its tension of opposites.

Oscillating between the two extremes of a polarity stretches us. As we learn about each side of ourselves, we gain experience in the reconciliation of duality. Eventually we learn to live from center, the "zero point" from which each pair of opposites is held equally in consciousness, and each side of a contrary is equally regarded as real.

For instance, we can love another madly and at the same time dislike aspects of the loved one's personality. Or, we can enjoy being a mother and still resent our child's demands. When we understand that opposites can exist simultaneously, we stop pretending and learn to live within our incongruities without being out of balance or out of touch. We feel the tension from both sides at once, letting each be. This middle point is not a "neutral" place, but one of dynamic tension. Its energy is the intensity of bliss—anticipation and joy, the fullness of being alive.

A healthy ego knows how to embrace this tension; a needy ego often cannot withstand the pressure. It will, instead, look for a simplistic solution and settle into a one-sided opinion. There it will try to rest convinced, committed to convincing others to share its view in order to feel secure. When we find ourselves denying ambiguities and resting in a single-minded viewpoint, we've stalled our individuation process and won't move again until something gets shaken loose.

Being stalled is not even the worst thing that can happen. When we polarize ourselves into one side of any opposition and are unwilling to look at the other side, we create a psychic situation called *enantiodromia*: the psyche spontaneously swings us into a devastating experience of the side we've been unwilling to face. The preacher who harangues about the "sins of the flesh" is caught in the arms of a prostitute. The wife who blindly claims she has a "perfect marriage" finds herself in a miserable divorce battle.

The psyche, apparently, is not interested in perfection; it is interested in completion. The psyche wants to know the dark and the light, the lows and the highs, the human and the divine which make up its nature.

We've all got a recalcitrant part of the self who functions through fear and doubt. This *antithesis self* keeps the "fire by friction" burning brightly, forcing us to stay attentive. Our inner "sparring partner" seeks a worthy opponent and guards the gateway into new dimensions of the Self, not allowing us to pass through until we confront and deal with its energy.

The following imagery can help you recognize and befriend this antithetical self:

GUIDED IMAGERY:
BEFRIENDING YOUR SHADOW SELF

Find a quiet place to lie down and go inward for awhile. You may want to put on some quiet music. Take a few deep breaths and begin tuning out the outside world, going into that place where you can imagine.

Now, in your mind's eye, see yourself sitting in the middle of a room, looking at a trap door over in the corner . . . You can hear a noise coming from behind the trap door, and you know some part of you is living down in the basement underneath the floor, a part of you who doesn't want to come along now that you are progressing forward . . .

Gather the courage to walk toward the door, moving slowly and quietly so as not to disturb what's underneath. Notice how you feel as you move closer to the door . . .

As you approach, you notice on a shelf a candle and a violet cloak. Put on the cloak and light the candle to carry with you. Now, open the door and walk down the stairs . . . Notice how you feel . . . or what images appear . . .

You are peering into the dark basement now, calling out to whoever is there . . . See what happens, or who appears . . . (long pause) See your shadow in all its glory! Its manner of dress, its stance . . . Notice its qualities and how it is trying to relate to you . . . (pause) Get a strong sense of its essence . . .

Now, ask your shadow to come forward . . . Ask it to tell you what it wants from you . . . And take note . . . (pause) Ask it how long it's been with you, and what function it serves . . . (pause) Now, tell it what you want from it . . . And notice its response . . . (pause) Find a way to make a pact with your shadow to give each of you something you need from the other . . . (pause)

Allow your self and your shadow to relate, and see what comes from this spontaneously . . . End your encounter in a manner that pleases you . . . (pause) Then, gradually let the whole scene fade into a light gray mist, until you are once more sitting in the center of the room, contemplating your experience . . . (long pause)

Now, still retaining all that occurred in your subjective life, be aware that you are here in this reality. Take some time to come back fully, and then record your experience.

Awakening Imagination,
Inspiration, and Intuition

The intellect can by-pass wisdom and consciousness like a motorcyclist can a walker; it does so daily in every university.

—John Hitchcock, *The Web of the Universe*

As we step out of old ways of knowing, our higher human cognitions ignite. These cognitive powers exist on a mental plane beyond the intellect we generally use, which is associated with our personal ego. Powers of our archetypal Soul—*creative imagination, inspiration,* and *intuition*—activate within minds and hearts which are living in surrender to a Higher Order. These three aspects of the divine law of active intelligence are the ways your soul "thinks."

Your soul is your link between the spiritual and the material kingdoms. Consequently, it can "think" in both directions, as a divine being and as a human one. The archetypal Soul takes form in each of us as the human psyche, which serves as its mirrored reflection. When perceptually clear, our psyches "step down" the wisdom of spiritual realities into *thought forms* that we perceive through flashes of direct knowing and through images that appear in our minds. The stronger and more precise the image, the greater the likelihood that the image will "matter" and come true.

Future-making is a willed internal command, not a passive petition. Once a solid image or "knowing" comes to us from our inner life, we invoke spiritual intent in communion with what is unfolding from within and then put our energy behind it. When aligned with our Creator's Will, human will power can bring about manifested results.

Let's look more closely at these higher ways of knowing:

CREATIVE IMAGINATION

Creative imagination is the mental function that bridges the gap between the actual and the ideal that we seek. The inner imaging process is a vehicle that carries us across the threshold into whatever new life we "think up." Subjective vision will always be the first stage of any new materialization.

Higher creative imaginings do not emanate from our ego desires, nor are they fantasies. Guided by a Higher Order, creative imaginings are the soul's perception of its rich eternal life, truths that well up from the soul's memory bank. The roving thoughts and empty visions of fantasy, on the other hand, come from our ego needs and have no basis in Reality. We use fantasy images to avoid living our lives. They are psychological defense mechanisms that keep us preoccupied with the unreal. Fantasy is making up images and thoughts that carry us *out of* experiencing. Creative imagination invents ways *into* experiencing.

The archetypal Self is a creative "imagineer" which thinks in relation to our bigger story. Consider your dreams and you'll see that images appear in ways your ego brain would never have imagined. Why would your father come to you in a dream dressed like a clown with a garden hoe in one hand and a serpent in the other? Who created this image? And who created the dream image of the home you lived in as a child as a cathedral or as a garden with a dark brown patch of burned grass in its center? These images have rich metaphorical meaning that, when interpreted by you, bring Self-knowledge that completes you.

We do not arbitrarily create perceptions that arise from our inner imaging mechanism. Reality with a capital R creates them in us! These inner images, according to Carl Jung, are *a priori*, which means they exist naturally in our consciousness. They seek outlets for expression through us. In *Agni Yoga* there is a saying: "The imagination is but a memory of that which already exists."

Remember, however, that inner imaging is not seeing pictures in vivid technicolor as we do with our outer eyes. Often people will tell me, "I'm not capable of doing guided imagery." Erroneously, they believe they are not imaging. But we are all imaging constantly! We've simply not understood that the inner eye "sees" differently than does the outer eye. With the inner eye, thought-impressions formulate in the mind, and we get a momentary impulse of a message, feeling, or scene.

For example, if I ask you to tell me what your house looks like, you'll start to describe it to me. If I ask from what perspective you are seeing your house, the front or the side, close up or from a distance, you'll tell me exactly. Isn't this some kind of "seeing"? Try this experiment right now with something you are thinking about.

By paying attention to how our soul speaks through our inner imaging process, we are following the mystery as it unfolds within our spiritual life. As we become skilled at interpreting these inner messages, we develop an intimate relationship with our individual soul and, further, with the archetypal Soul of humanity. Such knowing expands us greatly. Could it be that the creative imagination is our guy wire leading us on course toward a future our Higher Self already planned—perhaps even before we were born?

INSPIRATION

Inspiration is a feeling state that accompanies creative imaging and the insights that come from inner work. When you are inspired, you "turn on" like a light bulb. An inspired idea compels us toward materialization like a magnet's pull. An aspect of our Higher Self's desire nature, inspiration does not feel like a temporary or imbalanced "high," but more like a motor driving you to express.

When you are inspired, you are affected by the

archetype Eros or Love. We are generally motivated only by the things that interest us, but when we fall in love with something or someone, we are on fire to do something. Aflame with desire, we have our strongest urges to create. This is the function Eros serves. When something takes on archetypal significance, things get exceedingly energetic and profound. If what we desire is part of the divine plan, we will be guided by the archetypes that characterize the creation we are making. We will know something magical is occurring, something beyond the ordinary.

INTUITION

Intuition is a direct knowing of Spirit. True intuition activates when our will is perfectly aligned with the will of a Higher Order. Then something "pops" into an instant knowing. To intuit something is to identify with it, and identification is communion. In order to intuit something, we must love it immensely; otherwise, there will be no desire to commune with it. Love will always be the vital element in any profound knowing. Intuition does not come from the subconscious individual mind or from stored racial memory. It drops in directly from the superconscious mind, from the omniscient Soul. We immediately recognize our knowing as the Truth.

Many people believe they are experiencing an intuitive hunch when what is really happening is that their lower desire nature wants something. "My intuition told me to buy this house." (When it was far too expensive for your real financial situation.) "My intuition told me to marry him." (When the fact that he was the best "catch" in the county was your true motive for tying the knot.) Intuition is much too spiritually exacting to play around with our ego's little desires. True intuition is a quiet knowing that does not go away.

The intellect that we generally access gathers and organizes data from the outer world for logical use in the present. It's very useful for this purpose, so we don't want to throw it away. However, the intellectual mind is not a creative mind; it cannot carry us forward into the future. It does not intuit the universal processes of the collective unconscious, nor does it envision or dream.

When we rely on it exclusively, the intellect becomes a repository of static information and memorized habit patterns that manifest in automatic responses that have lost their life force through endless repetition. When you become unclogged from these old patterns and allow the winds of Spirit to blow fresh air through your brain, you'll start to see the ideal mental images of your new life. At first, these images will appear vague, like fragments of visions that are hardly noticeable. Once you turn your attention toward them with reverence, however, they will come forth more readily. Then, you'll start to see how a little piece here and a little piece there have begun to manifest in your life.

We were all born with these higher cognitive skills in place. Children imagine beautifully. Remember how you used to pretend when you were a child? Sadly, too many of us were taught that pretending meant we were being lazy, fanciful, or disobedient. Sometimes we were even punished for day-dreaming.

Your creative imagination was most likely what kept you sane when you were a child. Our stuffed animals and other imaginary friends and protectors were our way of accessing the symbolic world, where animals behave like humans. Studying the way children relate to images led Jung to believe that we are born with a basic imaginal capacity.

As adults we've forgotten how significant the mental power of imaging truly is. We don't realize that this mysterious power of thought is *the formative intentional mental process that creates life*. And so we must make the effort to bring this higher cognitive ability back into a place of honor within our mental lives and learn to trust it once more. Trusting your inner "imagineering" is like reuniting with a wonderful old friend.

RETURNING TO OUR
ETERNAL BEGINNINGS

*Any form whatever, by the mere fact that it exists as
such and endures, necessarily loses vigor and becomes
worn; to recover vigor, it must be reabsorbed into the
formless if only for an instant; it must be restored to
the primordial unity from which it issued; in other
words, it must return to "chaos."*

—MIRCEA ELIADE, *The Myth of the Eternal Return*

Because we are connected to all that is, every
time we enter into making a new creation, we
must go back to our archetypal beginnings, the
origin time when all our activities were consecrated by
the gods.

Often, going back is helped by remembering our
biological birth and the family conditions into which
we were born. When we revisit our birth, we have the
opportunity to integrate and release any difficulties we
experienced and to disidentify from this aspect of our
"small story." Then, free of any negative conditioning
we took on during our gestation and birth, we can live
again in the natural purity and potential which is our
birthright.

Leonard Orr, one of the pioneers of the rebirthing movement, explains how rebirthing can heal us this way:

Rebirthing is unraveling the birth-death cycle, which means all conditioning. It's about being a conscious expression of the eternal Spirit, which means total healing and mastery.

I've experienced the rebirthing process myself and have participated in spontaneous rebirthing experiences with hundreds of people in Integrative Breathwork sessions during our healing programs. Working with the breath and with music, we relax into a meditative state and often find ourselves returning to our mother's womb. In soul-time, past, present, and future run together in what we might call "simultaneous reality." Rebirthing researchers and our own experience confirm that memories of our biological birth and even of our perinatal experiences exist just below the surface of our conscious awareness. While regressed, we can actually bring into the present what it felt like when we first incarnated here. We were conscious beings in the womb. The fetus encodes its learning through experiential data; it does not conceptualize as adults do.

Many people have asked me why is it so important for us to reexperience our birth. I often answer by pointing to how much I have learned about myself through my own rebirthing experiences. During one session, I found myself lying beside my mother's body repeating over and over, "No one here knows how to feed me." From this I learned that I came into this world as a spiritual being encoded with the sense of having arrived in a world devoid of spiritual food. Born two months premature, I was starving literally as well. I weighed less than four pounds and had been anesthetized. (My mother had been given ether.) My depressing start to life was captured perfectly by my spontaneous cellular memory.

During another session, I cried out, "I'm going to be lost! I'm going to be lost!" When I asked my mother about the meaning of this memory, I discovered that she had been wringing her hands all the way to the hospital, saying over and over, "Dear God, please don't let me lose my baby!" This fear that "I'll be lost" has followed me irrationally throughout my life. As long as I keep my precarious birth conscious, I'm okay. Otherwise these feelings of fragility overtake me at inopportune times and cause me to feel weak and little.

Another rebirthing experience taught me that I have come from the heaven worlds. As I was reliving coming through the birth canal, I felt that I was falling from heaven. I scribbled on a piece of paper, "I miss my Father!" Later, in processing this breathwork session, I realized it was my heavenly Father I had been missing! In my rebirthing, I had experienced "the Fall," a universal archetype available to us all. For years, I'd been aware of a vague sense of not wanting to be here. I felt that I'd never fully incarnated, believing there was nothing here that could "feed me." Remembering the heaven world and my heavenly Father, I was homesick for a better place.

Returning to these original birth experiences recalls our initiation from a watery world into an airy one. Our transformation from an aquatic creature to one which breathes air is the first instance of death and rebirth our body/ego experiences. The imprints birth leaves on our consciousness influence how we will react later in life to other transformational experiences. Though our original feelings may still come up, since the patterning laid down by our birth runs deep, bringing our birth process into conscious awareness in adulthood gives us the opportunity to make new decisions about how we will cope with change.

Until we make the patterns set up by our birth conscious, they have power over us. These old feelings are causative, and they affect decisions we make about life, often without our conscious knowledge.

So stop for awhile now and reflect on your own beginnings. Think, for instance, about the conditions that existed in your family when you were born. What was the relationship between your mother and father? Were you wanted? Was there disease or emotional discomfort present then? Was there abuse? What family issues can you name that may have affected your newborn self? What was your family's value system? Its religious attitude? What family codes had been handed down that you were to uphold? What were your family's weaknesses and its strengths? Who were your role models? What role did you play? Take some time to reflect on these questions now.

You can go even deeper. Find a quiet space and put

on some beautiful music that reminds you of birth. Go into a relaxed, non-ordinary state of consciousness for awhile and see what images come as you recall your beginnings here on planet Earth.

The following guided imagery will help you remember:

GUIDED IMAGERY:
REMEMBERING YOUR BIRTH

Close your eyes and take a few deep breaths . . . until you feel yourself slipping out of this outer reality, going inward to that place where you can imagine for awhile . . .

Begin to feel yourself encased in the warm, watery life of your mother's womb. Feel what it's like to be there in that space . . . safely floating . . . And hear the sounds . . . And note what images come . . . (long pause)

Now, feel the walls of your "house" becoming constricting . . . Tighter and tighter . . . You can hardly breathe! You've outgrown this space and it's no longer a safe place to be . . . Notice this shift as it begins to happen . . . (pause)

Then, it gets worse: The walls of your house are now rocking in waves of strong contractions . . . And listen to the sounds . . . as though an earthquake is happening, with you right in its midst! . . . Everything is changing now . . . You must get out or you will die . . . Let yourself feel this process of labor beginning . . . (pause) Allow the quality of this experience to penetrate your consciousness . . . (long pause)

Suddenly you are moving through a tunnel, heading toward a pinpoint of light you can barely perceive . . . Let yourself go toward the light . . . Feel the crushing suffocation as you enter fully into this remembrance of passing through the birth canal (remind yourself to keep breathing as you remember this stage) . . . Notice the images that appear . . . the feelings . . . the sounds . . . the messages you are giving yourself . . . Become your mother now, and notice what she's going through as you are born . . . the messages she is giving you . . . what her reality is like . . . (long pause)

And now, all tension is suddenly released . . . you're born . . . Notice what your first few moments in this reality feel like . . . the quality of this experience . . . (long pause) . . . the helpers, the terror, the love . . . whatever comes . . . Just be with these feeling for awhile and let yourself remember . . . (long pause)

Slowly, now, bring yourself back to your grown-up self, still recalling this original experience of being so new, so small . . . And allow these two realities to be as one. You are that little new one, and simultaneously, you are all grown up, able to nurture this blessed child who lives within your heart.

This process can make you feel very vulnerable and touched by the remembrance of yourself as a little newborn person. So take some time to really integrate this experience. It is a precious recollection.

As a practical mystic-in-training, you are becoming what's called a "twice-born" soul. You have been birthed from your mother's womb. Now, you are birthing yourself into your own Higher Self. Remaining consciously in a state of Self-remembrance of our double nature is the task of the today's mystic.

As twice-born builders of bridges into the coming world, we develop the double-vision awareness of the way-shower who walks in two worlds at once. We do our best to stand poised between the created past and the virgin world just ahead, willing to go through the winds of change in ways that befit spiritual beings incarnated in human form.

BRINGING ORDER OUT OF CHAOS

Rhythm beats deep in chaos patterning. Its music sings us into existence, body and soul. Following even just a couple of the major motifs in chaos theory will reveal the symphonic union between modern science and ancient mysticism.

—KATYA WALTERS, *The Tao of Chaos*

C haos is the creative force that provides the rich pool of unfolding potential we call "the future." The creative energy of chaos, spinning this way and that with no directive force, must be tapped and then expressed in ways that bring about order. This sounds very difficult. But there are principles that guide this process that we can use to manifest anything—from a project to a personal relationship.

The scientific understanding of chaos theory teaches us about the actual mechanics of how Spirit works to transform us. Borrowing the language of science to describe the mechanics of Spirit, here are the three steps in the process of bringing order out of chaos:

STEP 1: BIFURCATE

For something to manifest, it must split in two, or *bifurcate*. We encourage this doubling to occur by entering into the energy of a situation and becoming part of its dynamic. When we mirror the energy of what is unfolding, our reflection shapes what we are invoking into a usable pattern.

Two-ness creates a dynamic which makes relationship possible. Think of how many pairs we have found to be essential to the work of practical mysticism: the ego and the soul; the individual and the archetype; the shadow and the Self; the conscious and the unconscious mind; life's "little story" and its "bigger story." Without relationship, there can be no movement. The whimsical saying "It takes two to tango!" is actually a powerful cosmic rule!

STEP 2: OSCILLATE

Once there are two of anything, they begin to *oscillate*, or resonate with each other. You can picture oscillation as a figure 8 turned sideways, like the infinity sign in mathematics. Now, imagine energy running back and forth in the pattern of the figure 8, and you will see how Spirit (soul) and matter (ego) descend and ascend as they relate to each other. Oscillation continues until their natures match and the two mirror each other perfectly.

STEP 3: ITERATE

As this dance of two-ness continues, each side in

the dynamic learns from the other through *iteration*, or repetition. Then each side feeds back into the resonance the results of its own learning. Once the resonance pattern is harmonized or balanced, there is freedom to move on.

In our lives, we follow these three stages whenever we encounter something with which we wish to interact with the aim of transformation or creation. First, we open ourselves and enter a dynamic relationship with the other. Second, we stay clear, which means that we remember at all times who we are in our essential nature. Finally, we resonate in harmony with the other, blending into a mirrored image, until we come into complete rapport. This is the movement of your soul!

When we are unwilling to enter into dynamic relationship with an aspect of "otherness" in our lives, we risk becoming a pawn of forces we cannot control. Haven't we all experienced this? When we are in denial, refusing to deal with something important, what we are ignoring often takes us over and then, at some point, comes upon us like fate. When this happens, of course, we feel we are fate's victim.

But when we are willing to risk the chaos of the uncreated, our soul (energy) and our ego (matter) relate so that they can bring about inner transformation or outer manifestation. The boundary between chaos and order, between the unconscious and conscious minds, is where we meet the uncreated potentials which await entrance into the world of form.

Entering with courage into this dance of opposites can help us when we are torn by a difficult decision. Here's an example:

Say you've been feeling the need to change your profession. This is troubling because changing jobs threatens your need for security. The chaotic energies of confusion between these two needs keeps you awake at night. Though you try to avoid the situation by not thinking about it, you are stuck.

Then one night just before retiring, you ask your Higher Self to send you a symbol to show you how to proceed. For the next few nights you notice a recurrent image in your dream life: As you're walking through your house, a new hallway leading to a room you didn't know was there keeps showing up.

As you reflect on the images of your dream, your soul and ego are beginning to resonate. Your soul is saying, "There's another hallway in your house that leads to a new room." Your intellect listens to this metaphor and begins to feel assured. In spite of your doubts, you find the courage to enter the chaos of the unknown; you make the call to a friend who runs a job placement service, and this starts you on the path towards the wonderful new job that's out there for you. It's as though you actually grew into the person for the job by deciding to go forward!

As long as you tried to resolve your dilemma with your ego/intellect alone, you were stuck. Then, your soul brought you the energies of transformation that stirred your psyche into activity by keeping you awake, until one night, you "exploded" into dreaming. This was your soul's way of oscillating and iterating with your ego, until you began to resonate with dream images. Your practical ego and your soul began to dance. Through resonating with your soul's message, you created order out of chaos and, as if by magic, brought the perfect new job into being.

This inner dance of ego and soul is one kind of transformational resonance. However, for most of us, a meaningful relationship with another human being is a necessary aspect of wholeness and manifests the dance of two-ness. Perhaps you are longing for a teacher who will guide you in your spiritual work. Perhaps it's a partner you need, someone who will help balance your inner masculine and feminine principles.

The more we willingly delve into the chaos of our transformational processes and then open and share our experiences with others, the more quickly we realize that what we're used to calling "me" is a very limited version of our whole Self. When we surrender into relationship, it is as if a new archetype is being born. Every relationship is an opportunity to "follow the mystery." The following story demonstrates what I mean:

Say you are falling in love with someone, but she will not tell you what's going on with her. She is mysterious, yet compelling. She seems to like you, but you don't really know for certain how she feels. Perhaps she wants a relationship with you, but you've not been able to get her to speak about it.

Despite nothing being settled and there being no guarantees, you decide simply to surrender and let go of your need to know where you stand. You accept her as she is and try to resonate to her way of being.

Then one day, you find that the two of you have come into intimate rapport. Two bodies, two people, yet together as one. You notice how you flow back and forth, giving and receiving, with no interference from doubt or consternation about the future—just a deep sense of harmony. Now the time for declarations has arrived: she begins to tell you how much she loves you. Resonance has blossomed miraculously into mutual love.

What happened here? You did not try to manipulate her or to figure her out, to outsmart her or to make her your possession. Nor did you demand that she clarify her feelings. Instead, you simply accepted her as she is and learned over time to respond to her way of falling in love. Partnering with another so as to become the oscillating force that reflects for the other their soul is truly the highest kind of love!

The only way we can ever know anything is to become one with it. To do this, we must give up our usual ways of staying separate. The question is always this: Do we have the courage to let go and fall into something other than ourselves? This is the key to all true relating. Relationship is the only way your soul knows how to live.

When we rise to meet and mirror another person or an idea which is coming into consciousness, we bifurcate. Then, as we begin flowing and merging with the other's dynamics, we oscillate or resonate. As we absorb and reflect the energy of the other, or iterate, we become *the one that has split into two*. This is love in action.

This mutual sharing of Spirit with matter weaves something uncreated into a greater and greater symmetry. A third and higher thing has been created and evolution marches on. Two-ness is a sacred function. To know union, we must first know duality.

The following guided imagery will help you enter into a dynamic relationship with the chaos that initiates transformation:

GUIDED IMAGERY:
STANDING ON THE PRECIPICE

Close your eyes and go into that place where you can imagine, allowing your outer reality gently to fade. You might want to take ten or so deep breaths to go into a timeless state more easily. You might also want to play some music without words to deepen your experience.

In your mind's eye, see yourself walking down a lovely path on a beautiful sunlit day. Notice your surroundings as you walk along. Feel yourself into this scene . . . (pause)

As you look ahead, you notice someone is coming toward you . . . someone who seems vaguely familiar, who reminds you of yourself . . . Notice that the two of you begin to mirror and reflect one another as you come closer together . . . As if by magic, you find you can move into and out of each other with ease . . . Notice how this feels . . . (pause)

You understand now that this other is your own soul! Take a moment to feel the joy of this conscious reunion! . . . And now, listen carefully to what your soul has come to say. It is an inspired message about your immediate future, so take heed . . . (long pause)

And now that you've captured the message, you notice that the two of you, as one, are standing on the edge of a precipice . . . looking out over the giant Void . . . See this place in your mind and feel your way into it . . . (pause)

Now, with a deep breath and a great sense of courage, step into the Void . . . And see what happens! . . . long pause)

The image now begins to fade into a light gray mist, and you are once more walking along the beautiful path . . . contemplating this experience you just had with your soul. Still retaining all that just happened subjectively, bring yourself back to your usual place in this ordinary reality, and take some time to integrate this experience. You might want to move around a little to feel yourself back in your body.

Be sure and write down or draw whatever message you received. Pay special attention to what you experienced when you stepped into the Void. This process is like dreamwork: it's liable to fade and you may not remember it later. Take your time before you resume any regular activity. This may have been a powerful experience!

LIVING THE SYMBOLIC LIFE

A genuine symbol is the expression of a spontaneous experience that points beyond itself to a meaning not conveyed by a rational term . . . It is an expression of something superhuman and only partly conceivable. It may be the best expression possible, yet it ranks below the level of the mystery it seeks to describe.

—CARL JUNG, *Psychology and Religion: West and East*

Symbols are our agents of transformation. In the symbolic world we meet our incoming future Self and the life it will weave around itself. Symbols come from the higher world closer to the Source. They carry us across the threshold into the new life that awaits us.

Symbols are not simply entertainment for our brains; nor are they mere representations. *Symbols are highly potent powers* that function as messengers for the greater "something" that stands behind them—something so big we scarcely even imagine it: *the mystery of You!*

Your psyche, as the mirrored reflection of your soul, speaks to you through images, symbols, metaphor, allegory, myth, and intuitive hunches. Your psyche "talks" through these mediators. The messages your psyche provides through these means always relate to the needs of your whole personality, because your soul knows everything there is to know about you!

Dream images are a good example. They come without notice, outside of your conscious control, giving you messages you never could have invented through your calculating brain. Dream symbols "step down" abstract spiritual forces by giving us something we know how to define. For example, say we dream of a shovel; well, we know what shovels are generally used for. Say we "receive" an image of the Fool or another known archetype. There are many books we can consult that will help us interpret universal symbols such as those in the Tarot or in world mythology.

If a symbol comes to you that you do not understand and have no logical way of interpreting, just wait. Eventually your psyche will bring you an interpretation. Otherwise, the image would not have been sent to you. Sometimes symbols are "previews" through which our psyche is preparing us for a coming change. Sometimes some aspect or quality in ourselves or our lifestyle must shift before we can take in this new information. So be patient with yourself.

Your psyche is your *autonomous pattern of wholeness*. Its deepest desire is to keep you connected to your whole story. It is the storehouse of all you've ever been and yearn to be. You can always go inward, even for only a moment, and retrieve a symbol that will provide an instant snapshot of this wholeness. Try this now, and you'll see:

EXERCISE: RETRIEVING AN IMAGE OF WHOLENESS

Close your eyes and take a deep breath. Ask your psyche to send you a symbol that represents the Self that is wanting to express through you right now . . . (pause) Take whatever symbol comes, no matter how irrational it may seem, and place it in your heart. Feel it coming into your body as a new "organ" you are to accept and learn to live into . . .

Make careful note of the qualities of this symbol, for you are now to be the bearer of this new or deeper Self you are becoming . . . First, name these qualities . . . (pause) Now, take them in . . . And feel yourself as this new one . . . Notice how you feel as you take in this higher identity . . . Now, commit to making these new qualities a part of your life from now on . . .

Take some time to imagine yourself walking around in your life as this new Self . . . and anchor this sense as your new reality . . . (pause)

Now, still retaining all that just happened inwardly, come back to this reality. Draw the symbol you received or describe it in writing, along with any important insights you may have received . . .

If you cannot understand as yet what the symbol means, be patient. Your answer will come when you are ready to take responsibility for representing it. Remember, we are only given as much Reality at any moment as we can stand!

Once recognized and entered into with a keen awareness, the symbolic life brings us intuitive realizations, fills in the gaps that leave us bleak or confused, and floods our lives with a sense of sacred purpose.

I am reminded of a story about Professor Abraham Maslow, the father of self-actualization theory. When he was standing in a long line to receive his diploma in psychology at an esteemed university gathering, he noticed how uncomfortable and silly he felt wearing a wide square hat and dark heavy robe. But as he looked down the line of those who were standing there similarly dressed, his perception suddenly shifted. Viewed through an archetypal lens, he saw himself standing in a succession of the great scholars of human history, himself an individual link in that honorable lineage. A thrill spread throughout his body, and his mind became reverent and alert.

We, too, can access such moments of greatness and meaning in our daily affairs. As we have learned, transformation requires that we enter fully into a dynamic relationship with a person or idea so that we can resonate with it. The same rule applies to interpreting symbols and dream images. We cannot remain outside the image as a remote, disinterested spectator. The key to awakening to a higher level of consciousness is our ability to experience our subjective life *as a felt reality*.

Interpreting a symbol means opening to its energy on every possible level. Keeping a dream journal, dialoguing with the images and symbols that come, drawing them, writing about them, dancing with them in your objective and subjective worlds will reveal much about them and about you.

Remember, however, that when you are working with symbols, you cannot always expect to find a single or simple interpretation. In the symbolic world, Truth exists on many levels simultaneously. We must learn to work with paradox and be comfortable with ambiguity. "Uniformity of meaning robs the mystery of its darkness and sets it up as something that is known," Jung once said.

Symbols give us a complex and realistic picture of our wholeness. But be prepared for adventure! Just a brief meeting with your awesome archetypal Self can be a shock that shatters your illusions about reality!

WORKING WITH SYMBOLS

Paradoxically, although the unconscious is the vehicle through which transformational symbols come into being, symbols coming into form must be recognized and reflected upon consciously before they can do their work. Daily spiritual practice is necessary to keep our unconscious and conscious minds speaking to each other.

Symbols we can work with are coming to us all the time. When we repress the energy of our higher evolutionary impulses, or when our ego needs to heal a wound, intensity builds up, until the psyche pops open and an image presents itself. Symbols appear in our night world, in a daydream, or in a time of meditation or deep contemplation.

And you don't have to wait for a dream to appear. Symbolic images can be encouraged consciously through processes such as guided imagery, meditation, trance dancing, musical breathwork journeys, deep hypnotic states, or Jungian dreamwork. Those of you who are artists, dancers, musicians, poets, or practitioners of other creative arts know how your work often brings symbols into conscious awareness. But it is not necessary to be a talented artist to be a practical mystic. You can invent your own system.

My method is to keep a journal to record my insights, feelings, upsets, warnings, images, wishes, and invocations. A journal is not a diary, a place to record the things that happen as ordinary routine. Rather, it's a ongoing chronicle of a spiritual quest, with special attention to the images and symbols that are the psyche's gift. In the next chapter, I explain my technique for keeping a spiritual journal.

If you're willing, stop right now and make a firm decision that you will not let another day go by without beginning such a process! You must make a commitment. You can begin by invoking the decision to bring your unconscious and conscious minds together allowing them to become reacquainted, like long-lost pals. Marshall the powers of your creative imagination; you will be surprised at the rapid results once a commitment is made.

When we link symbols to life experiences, we are spiritualizing matter, bringing two levels of consciousness together, like overlapping circles. The meeting place in the middle is a potent gateway between dimensions.

Communicating with a symbol and getting in touch with its transformational energy is a three-stage process:

STEP 1: MEET

Whether you meet a symbol in a dream, an imagery process, or a highly charged conscious waking state, the first step is to see it in your mind as an object, something you can picture and name. Examine the symbol and draw a picture of it. By these actions, you are materializing the symbol, bringing it into form through the process of recognition.

As you examine or draw a symbol, it will begin to have an impact on your consciousness. Let your imagination run. You may feel sometimes that you are making up meanings, and that's okay. We actually make everything up. Modern physicists would agree that what we observe and call "reality" is in fact, our subjective reality. The action of observing something, changes it. If a symbol came out of your mind, it's yours to know. Use free association, and let yourself go.

STEP 2: MEDITATE

Next, begin reacting to the symbol. Think about it. Feel it. See how it affects you. Note things about it. Sum up your associations and insights into something orderly you can put into words, move to, draw pictures of, make a mask of, or otherwise work with. You are taking the symbol in, feeling yourself into it, merging with it so you can know it and assign it meaning. The symbol is now giving you its qualities that come from a Higher Order. This is the stage of *input*.

STEP 3: MEDIATE

Now, apply the symbol. If it's a symbol of the Self, become it. No longer reacting to the symbol, now you are resonating with it. You bring its qualities or insights into your daily life and direct its use or purpose fully. Make the meaning of the symbol manifest by moving with it spiritually to embody it. In other words, you are now the symbol's representative, a bridge between two worlds. This is the *output* stage. Now the particular quality or aspect of this symbol has come into being, through you.

To exemplify how this process works, I'd like to share a recent experience I had with a symbol at one of our workshop intensives. I had taken part in a mask-making exercise. When I returned to the art room to look at the clay and paper maché mask I had made, I was shocked. I had thought I was making the face of a woman, but what I saw was a Christ-like face similar to the one on the Shroud of Turin!

I was quite upset. I knew we were to do a mask ceremony later in the week during which I would have to portray my mask. Since I "knew" I had no way to be Christ, I went into an avoidance pattern and refused to work further on my mask.

For several days I scooted past the art room, unable to face my creation. Then, in desperation, because the ceremony was looming, I returned to the mask and sprayed colored ink over the face. The ink ran down the forehead like blood, making the face of Christ seem even sadder! I decided then I would find a green bush with berries to make a crown for the mask, to replace the ugly crown of thorns. It seemed the least I could do. Still troubled, I put off this task as well. Although I was avoiding conscious interaction with the symbol, disturbing dreams indicated that I was meditating on it at deep unconscious levels.

The night of the ceremony arrived. Fifteen minutes before it was to begin, I was outside in the dark in a rainstorm with a pair of scissors, searching for a bush. In the corner of the yard, I found one, and without being able actually to see it, I cut a branch.

When I put the crown on my mask, one of my friends remarked, "How interesting, Jacquie. That branch is from a hawthorne bush. See the berries?"

I was blown away! The crown that Jesus wore at Golgotha was made of hawthorne.

Finally, it was my time to go on stage to represent my mask. With as much bravery as I could muster, I put on the mask, faced the audience, and began repeating in a tentative whisper, "I am the way, the truth, and the life." My words had no energy. I was stuck. What right did I have to attempt this?

Then, spontaneously, without conscious thought, I slipped the mask to one side, so that my face was showing beside it. Then, through my tears, I began to sing Mary Magdelene's plaintive love song from *Jesus Christ Superstar*, "I Don't Know How to Love Him."

I had become Mary Magdalene, sorrowing over her inability to love Christ properly. I had embodied the meaning of a symbol by manifesting the shadow side of a profound archetype that is a part of every woman. In becoming a living representative of the symbolic world and bridging it with my real human life, I felt I was healing an important part of myself— and perhaps—transforming the archetype as well!

A PRACTICAL MYSTIC'S
RULES OF THE ROAD

The moment one definitely commits oneself, then Providence moves too. All sorts of things occur to help one that never otherwise would have occurred . . . Whatever you can, do. Or dream you can, do. Begin it. Boldness has genius, power and magic in it. Begin it now.

—GOETHE

Discovering the power you have as a human soul can be disconcerting at first. You come to understand that you must take full responsibility for your thoughts, emotions, and actions, at all times. An awakening Self can no longer be irresponsible. An awakening Self can no longer blame others or "fate" for what transpires. You have committed to evolve. You have decided to go Home.

But we must become skilled travelers on the path of awakening. The practical mystic's rules of the road are really just logical psychological and spiritual truths. If we follow them, our transition to the next stage of development will be more graceful.

RULE ONE

Be a responsible steward of your energies. Trust your intuition to know when to take on greater responsibilities and when to pull back or slow down.

When your energies are too expanded, you will feel "high" or out of control. Though high energy feels good, it may not lead to the best outcomes. You'll tend to see things only in their positive aspect and won't recognize their shadow side until it's manifesting in ways that harm.

You may sense over-expansion in your body as shortness of breath, rapid speech, or too much talking. When you become aware that this is happening, slow down, breathe, and use your will to come into a calmer state that is more contained and alert.

When your energies are too contracted, you may feel it in your chest as a constricted or closed heart. Depression or a loss of interest in life often accompanies this state. Decisions you make during times of contraction might, in retrospect, seem short-sighted or lacking in creativity. To overcome contracted energy, go within and see what emotions you might be repressing.

Both over-expansion and contraction can be the result of too little rest, not enough exercise, missed meals, or the wrong diet. We learn the right use of energies through practice. Depletion is never appropriate. No matter how intense our schedule, we can find a rhythm in our days.

RULE TWO

Strive to develop a new rhythm that befits your evolving soul. As you enter into a new frequency of awareness, your body, emotions, and mental life will all be affected. You are entering a whole new field of experience.

Your body's energies may be charged with fire. Your emotions may shift rapidly from high to low. Your mind may vacillate between confidence and doubt, clarity and confusion. These alterations indicate that a refining process is going on, until you become anchored in your highest truth as your new and more permanent condition.

To cope with these swings, try to keep in mind the Hermetic maxim: *Energy follows thought.* Clear your mind of its unnecessary chatter and your mental energies will naturally smooth out. Conscious attention to self-nurturing will help balance your physical state. Watching your emotional alterations without following them into extreme highs and lows will keep your emotions in steady rhythm.

Waking up to our greater life is not an easy task. Nor are the birth pangs of the world's current millennial transition without pain. We all have much unlearning to do.

As you become more proficient in the ways of the practical mystic, you will learn to remain inwardly peaceful, as though in deep meditation, as you travel through your days. Meditation means staying in touch with your inner Self, not only through the passive form of sitting in silence. Perhaps you were trained in former lifetimes through such discipline, and you are now able to walk around "seeing double," as if constantly in a state of open-eyed meditation. Practical mystics cultivate a rhythm between inward stillness and outward activity in whatever way is appropriate.

RULE THREE

Travel the evolutionary path as a soul-dominated personality. Cultivate the soul awareness to become proficient at the following important tasks:

•*Surmounting personal problems.* Be willing to reenter the past to "cook" your "uncooked seeds" without shame or blame. It's not easy to face the chaos of unfinished personal business or an unconscious complex, but only by doing so can you bring a problem to consciousness so it can release.

Anytime you get out of balance, you'll feel suffering in your heart, the bridge between your lower and higher bodies. When you feel your heart activating, it often means you are "cooking." Perhaps deep grief, resentment, depression, a need to cry out or to be enraged needs to be released.

Practical mystics learn to "bleed these feelings out" in a safe and appropriate setting. Sometimes I'll get into my car, roll up the windows, turn on music, and drive down a country road wailing, chanting, or toning—anything to open my throat and let the feelings out.

When we enter this stage of our awakening, the shadow may become more pronounced. Be prepared for this. Remember, the brighter the light, the greater the shadow! Shadow work is crucial, for whatever we do not integrate will follow us relentlessly into our new life, there to manifest itself in some new way.

- *Bringing your thoughts under control.* Be willing to watch what you let come into your mind and then react to. As we practice "changing our minds" we must again and again be willing to face the opposites that confront us. Living in paradox is more real than trying to find a simple, one-sided solution. Remember *enantiodromia*! If you cling too hard to one side of an opposition, your psyche will revert to the side that is being denied and teach you a hard lesson.

- *Differentiating between ego reactions and soul responses.* When in doubt about whether a response is from your ego or your soul, remember that your ego will generally be on the side of personal gratification. "What's in it for me?" the ego asks. Your soul, on the other hand, is group-oriented and will generally be on the side of whatever is good for the whole. Your soul seeks to serve humankind with the same zest as the ego seeks to gratify itself!

As you make the transition from your old state to a new state of being, you'll find that the "stuff" of your personal biography often stands in the way of complete Self-remembrance. For the one Soul of humanity to embody in us, it must fight its way through the debris belonging to our ego personality. Therefore there simply must be a confrontation! Embodying the soul takes a great deal of purification and deep inner work. You will feel your soul's influence first in your thoughts, then in your emotions. Finally you will behave as a soul-dominated personality in your everyday reality.

RULE FOUR

Live as an embodied soul in all your activities. Your soul has many wonderful qualities. See how many of them you can activate in your life as a soul-dominated personality:

- Purity of motive.
- Harmlessness in thought, speech, and action.
- Balance and poise.
- Authenticity of expression and action.
- Spontaneous and playful delight.
- Heightened senses, including supersensible ones.
- Self-awareness.
- Tranquility and inner silence.

Make a commitment to find a structured way to develop any of these qualities you lack.

Once you start to become conscious, there are no more excuses and no turning back. You can practice the principles suggested here or make up your own, until you become proficient at being a soul-dominated personality. When you see that you've "slipped" (as we all do from time to time), instead of blaming yourself, simply *observe* your behavior without judging and come back to true.

Becoming defensive when you feel confronted will also no longer work. Anytime you catch yourself being defensive, drop it, and see what happens. Your worst fear is that you'll be shown to be a fool. Pride is often our strongest vice. Yet, when we drop our defensive posture, the very opposite of what we expect often occurs. You may discover that "giving in" is actually enjoyable. You'll learn much about yourself, and your relationships will become more loving, less tense, more intimate. After all, you are learning to live in surrender to a Power greater than you. It's only fitting that you take off your armor and leave your weapons at the door!

This process of individuation is notorious for its trials. The main hindrances are two: First, the work of practical mysticism is unfamiliar to the Western mind, which has traditionally been invested in a materialistic outlook. Second, we Westerners are predisposed to over-development of the analytical left brain, which blocks intuition and the inner life.

These hindrances will try to slow down your growth. Be aware that you will not receive a great deal of support for your new ways of thinking or being. Rather, you must become self-sufficient through observation, inner psychological work, study, honest dialogue with brothers and sisters on the path, and meditation. Committed work on yourself *is* your new service to humankind!

Now that you have made a commitment to growth, keep in mind that you will receive a wealth of information from dreams, insights, visions, or inspirations. Take note, be patient with yourself, and keep rubbing the sleep from your eyes!

Here are a few techniques for overcoming hindrances you'll meet on the path:

- Make hindrances conscious as they appear, with no sense of shame.

- Do the next right thing that comes along.

- Cultivate humility and dispassion. Being dispassionate does not mean being cold, aloof, and unfeeling; rather, it's dropping your investment in getting your way. Relax as much as possible and undergo whatever temporary inconvenience you must while holding in view the future you are invoking. Learn what you can from each encounter.

- Synthesize opposites. The "middle path" always leads straight to the heart. Accept and harmonize ambiguity and paradox. Remember that no situation is ever black and white, except while opposites have split apart so they can each be seen clearly. "Two-ness" is a temporary state—a psychological function that indicates that something is in the process of being created. Always go toward that third and higher thing that takes in both sides.

•Don't use positive thinking to block shadows that need to be faced. Positive thinking makes the mind receptive to right action. It holds the "good" inside, even when things are going badly outside. Soul-dominated individuals work within the tension of positive and negative thoughts. Trying to be "positive only" will always backfire.

•Learn to let go gracefully while the one Soul of humanity works through you. Cultivate a willed spontaneity. As you become more transparent, energies from the higher worlds are able to penetrate more easily to do the work of Spirit.

•Honor moments of intuitive knowing as magical times. Every image that emerges from your unconscious mind is important. Keep a dream notebook beside your bed. Realizations can happen at any time. Be ready to receive them.

Maintaining the proper discipline of Self-remembrance will help when we feel pulled apart by the demands of a conscious spiritual life. The interior work of holding the vision while doing what needs to be done in all our relations in the outer world demands that we be vigilant and strong-hearted. Yet this work of bringing our inner and outer lives into balance is the most profound work we can undertake!

A New Dispensation
Comes with Every Age

Robbed of its mystical tradition, an outer system is like a rose perfume.

—CAITLIN MATTHEWS, *The Western Way*

A t the dawning of every age, we open a fresh petal of God's flower. Every age is a training ground in which humanity learns an aspect of its divine nature. The new quality we are called to develop becomes the keynote for a cycle of time. While a keynote is active, we absorb that quality. Ultimately, we become the quality and are able to use it to better ourselves and all humankind.

The keynote for the Piscean Age we are leaving is Devotion. This quality of Soul has taught us how to worship and to foster visions that inspire us passionately enough to involve us completely. When we worship something, we are magnetized by its image. When we send this image our emotional and mental energy, it reciprocates. As we literally "look up to it," what we worship lifts our vibration to its frequency.

The new quality that is the keynote of the dawning Aquarian Age is Self-Creative Expression. Aquarius is the "water-bearer" who nourishes our world by abundantly "spilling over" with gifts of Spirit. Aquarian energy frees us to focus attention on Self-advancement. It calls us to turn inward and learn to materialize the visions fostered during the Age of Devotion. We are to focus now on recognizing and developing our *own* talents and potential.

The most difficult part of any cycle, of course, is the ending, when two keynotes overlap. At such times, crosscurrents and chaos are the norm. The great esoteric philosopher Rudolf Steiner pointed out that at the close of any century, humanity's leading edge will be the "cross-over" people, strong souls who carry the seeds of the next stage of human evolution. For us, this is doubly significant, for we face not simply the end of a century, but the closing of an Age! Think what this means for all of us who are feeling drawn to awaken. We are earmarked for the struggles of the birth of a new humankind. You might say that we are pregnant with new life.

Practical mystics of the Aquarian Age will be the builders of the visions fostered in the Piscean Age now passing. We will also be called to release the misuses of worship and devotion, including fanaticism, elitism, bigotry, and narrow-mindedness. Instead of worshiping the scientific view of what life is, for example, we'll seek a deeper reverence for *divine revelation* as a way of guiding humanity.

As we prepare for the coming Age, the seeming oppositions on which we based our understanding—soul vs. body, Spirit vs. matter, subjective vs. objective, East vs. West, divine vs. human—are beginning to dissolve for us. A new wholistic consciousness whose impulse is synthesis is coming into being. We're expanding to see that we are *both* human and divine.

As we look ahead, we can look forward to the day when the inner life will be validated as real and the Soul language of illumination will be kitchen table talk. No longer will we be held hostage to the limited view of fact as dogma. Nor will we feel we must keep our spiritual lives a secret. The magical life will return, and we will, once and for all, become free thinkers who follow the mystery, capable of using with validity our soul's creative abilities to bring us closer to the Source.

So here we stand at the ending of the 1990s, vulnerable, curious, and somewhat tentative. We're being asked to do what humans fear the most: to live in the unknown, with no clue to what's coming next! Yet, there's a sense of exhilaration that makes this a time of enchantment and high spirits. As the intensity builds, we know that we're on the brink of something vastly important and that we are its harbingers.

Putting the exercises that follow into your life will keep you grounded in Self-remembrance and help you strengthen the courage to be all that you can be. As your process of individuation unfolds, you'll find that you stand in an energy field of raw, unbridled truth. Others will naturally begin to change and grow in your presence. These exercises will help you remember that it's not what you know but who you are that creates the magical space for Spirit to do its work.

EXERCISE: I AM WILLING!

Begin each day standing for just a moment or two in an erect, open position, facing the sky—with your feet apart and your hands above your head, making a V-shaped arrow-like directive stance toward the heavens. Your body will have made itself into the shape of an X. Make an invisible circle around you with the meaning that this is sacred space.

Now, with full intention, even with powerful feeling, cry out (either silently or aloud), "I AM WILLING . . . !" Maintain this stance for a moment or two while the energy takes hold . . . Then, emphatically draw your arms back down to your sides and consciously dissipate the invisible circle in your mind. Once this activity is completed, move away, and go about your business.

You needn't obsess about what is to come as an answer, for this represents a lack of faith. You've turned it over to your Higher Power. So you "let go and let God," relaxing as much as you can, willing to remain consciously aware of what comes as the response.

EXERCISE: KEEPING A
SPIRITUAL JOURNAL

The most powerful inner work I've done over the past twenty years has been keeping a spiritual journal. It records my revelations, inspirations, poetry, artwork, invocations, even quotations I come across that pertain to my greater story. I only document what is essential—the times when I know some major soul event is taking shape in my life.

I've seen how I have been individuating, recognizing and wrestling with my shadow, finding the inner Beloved, blending much of my masculine and feminine selves, becoming more mature and less reactive, and coming upon my true life's work with more willingness to express it—all this through the journaling and artistic processes that have come from interacting with my unconscious mind.

It is very important to date every entry. When you look back, you will see so clearly how your soul's journey through time unfolds along a larger trajectory than one mere ego's biography. You may have past life recalls, mystical experiences, or "big" dreams that are prophetic; or you may be able to chart how your invocations are always answered over time.

But when one event happens when you are twenty-nine, is not picked up again consciously until you are thirty-three, and not again until you are forty-two—of unfolding story line if you were attempting to recall it through your ordinary memory.

As mine has been, your spiritual journal will become your most cherished companion and will be a constant recorder of the fact that "you are more than what you look like."

EXERCISE: HONORING
THE PASSING OF THE DAY

Just before you retire each evening, ten to fifteen minutes of quiet reflection on the events of the day will help you hold the energies of transformation in reverence and keep your process of growth on track. You may wish to record your reflections in your spiritual journal.

Reflect on the events of the day, starting with the present moment and working backwards to the day's beginning. As you review events, many things that happened will pass right by with no particular energy attached. But now and then, something that happened will stop you, and you'll find you're caught up in trying to complete some conversation or relive some experience that was difficult to integrate. Your response means there's still energy in this event that needs to be released.

Remember what you know now about ordering

chaos. Completion requires that you face square-ly a piece of unfinished business. In other words, go back into it and feel yourself bringing forward what needs to be noticed, honored, perhaps cor-rected, and released. Be alert to images and sen-sations that arise as you reenter the scene. Be patient as the hidden dynamics of the situation reveal themselves. Ask yourself, what image is suggested by this event? What archetype was invoked? Make an honest attenpt to see the event plainly, with no judgment, shame, or blame. Just observe. Then, once this work is done, see the event fading into a light gray mist and let it go.

When you have worked your way backwards in this way to the beginning of the day, take some time to recall the sacred purpose you invoked that morning and whether the events of the day contributed to its unfoldment. If you find your invocation not bringing forth fruit, invoke your sacred purpose again as you go into the night world of sleep and dreaming. Doing so will help you clear your subconscious mind so that your dream life will come alive with inspired messages about your bigger story.

Honoring the passing of each day brings rev-erence and ritual to living and makes human life a sacred passage through time. It gives you a need-ed container for your experiences that keeps you protected—like an alchemical vessel, or the

Grail—so that Spirit can do its work of growing you whole without so much contamination and delay.

After you have worked with this practice for a while, you will find it to be so useful, you'll want to design your own modifications or additions.

As we come to the end our time together, let's bring home through symbol a message from your future:

GUIDED IMAGERY:
A FUTURE MEMORY

Find a quiet place where you can go inward for awhile, and move a wide searchlight back over your past. Take a look at your whole life from the overview. You may want to use some meditative music for this experience.

Begin by picturing yourself led by a wise being with a lantern who is guiding you down some steps into your past . . . carefully reminding you that you are safe, and can return anytime you wish . . . So you begin to image yourself walking down these stairs into your own past . . .

See what clues you get concerning any unfinished business you may have with someone, with yourself, or in some event . . . Notice the insult or the wounds . . . See the strengths that were present to meet the challenge . . . Be as objective as you can. And if a feeling comes up, go deeper! Let the feeling intensify . . . Give it your full intention, even exaggerate it somewhat, so you can really get into it and feel it through . . . (pause). This is a reactivity . . . some old complex is rising out of the chaos to be 'seen' . . . Take some time to let it be . . . to be with it . . . So you can know it . . . and it can thereby release . . . (long pause)

Continue doing this until you've passed back over your life . . . and see what comes up spontaneously . . . (long pause)

Now, with your inner eye, see yourself as you are today, in your current life experiences . . . (pause) Reflect on how far you've come from all that's passed . . .

Now, experience yourself turning in a forward direction, leaving your past behind . . . And notice how this feels . . . (long pause).

And see yourself in your mind's eye walking toward your future . . . Begin to feel yourself moving out of this ordinary time into the timeless world of the uncreated . . . And note what you see and experience that is trying to take form . . . The quality of your life as it changes into this timeless world . . . The quality of your current identity . . . See any images or symbols that want to reveal themselves to you . . .

And you are suddenly aware that your Future Self is walking toward you . . . Coming closer now, you can see this more completed Self . . . Note what you see . . . The quality of this identity . . . The quality of your relationship to your coming Self . . .

And now, just be with your Ideal Self for awhile . . . Merge into it and mirror it as best you can . . . And let it speak with you from within your own mind and heart . . .

Let it offer you a symbol of itself for you to place in your heart, and tell you from whence you've come . . . It will now give you an essential sense, a "flavor" or image of your greater Self, reminding you of your reason for this incarnation . . . Take this in with gratitude . . . (long pause)

Now, let it speak to you of your future life . . . and see what comes . . . (long pause)

As this image recedes and the energy subsides, you'll begin to come back into this ordinary reality. Take some time to write, draw, or integrate this experience for awhile before doing anything else.

EPILOGUE

Everything that happens here on earth is the materialization of a complete, accomplished cause waiting on the spiritual plane to materialize. When one achieves the ability consciously to reach the depths of the Self . . . we experience cause simultaneously with its effect—the future as a complete and perfect present.
—ELISABETH HAICH, *Initiation*

W hen our past and future come together, we remember who we are. When we focus our attention inwardly on a regular basis, we gradually learn to accept the fact that "the Theosophia of the gods," lives right inside our minds and hearts. To realize this gives our inner life an incredible depth and breadth!

Living with the "double vision" of those who can rise above their conditions while simultaneously fully entering into them, we are doing the work of the higher worlds that we came here to do. We activate the archetypal energy patterns down here on earth which produce a high state of emotional tension, a charged aliveness. It is during these charged times that we say

"Good heavens! I just dreamed about this last evening." Or, "Look at this miracle! Could this be chance, or does it have a special significance for me?" Our observation of their similarity of meaning is that "third element" beyond the two simultaneous events. And for the moment, we are a representative of the archetypal transpersonal Self, living beyond all appearances of duality. This brings together psyche and matter, the unconscious and conscious minds. There is no longer a space between our divine and mundane lives, as they have arranged themselves into a meaningful wholistic symmetry.

When we are in this unitary consciousness, we are living in the one real world, Carl Jung's *unus mundus*. We've stepped into the World of Meaning, which is the causative dimension of consciousness, our home base, where we can materialize Spirit. From this higher world, everything is revealed through the lens of its symbolic purpose for our lives, and for the life of humanity as one Soul. This is the state of Self-realization. It is the New Earth, and we, its remarkable inhabitants! Our recognition of it and willingness to "play the game" make it so.

QUEST BOOKS
are published by
The Theosophical Society in America,
Wheaton, Illinois 60189-0270,
a branch of a world organization
dedicated to the promotion of the unity of
humanity and the encouragement of the study of
religion, philosophy, and science, to the end that
we may better understand ourselves and our place in
the universe. The Society stands for complete
freedom of individual search and belief.
For further information about its activities,
write, call 1-800-669-1571, or consult its Web page:
http://www.theosophical.org

The Theosophical Publishing House
is aided by the generous support of
THE KERN FOUNDATION,
a trust established by Herbert A. Kern
and dedicated to Theosophical education.

ADVANCE PRAISE FOR
BECOMING A PRACTICAL MYSTIC

"Jacquelyn Small's extraordinary insight into ordinary
events and her compassionate nature make her an able
guide for those of us learning to wake up. I've made many
of her exercises a regular part of my daily meditation
practice—with profound results."

> —LINDA SPARROWE, contributing editor of *Yoga
> Journal* and author of *Women's Guide to Yoga*

"Here is the missing link between a commitment to the
spiritual life and bringing that commitment into everyday
living. From her own experience, Jacquelyn Small shares
what she knows about the power of Intention and Action to
transform the self and the world."

> —JUNE SINGER, PH.D., author of *Boundaries of
> the Soul*

"Jacquelyn Small is a consistent, reliable guide on the
spiritual path."

> —*Science of Mind* magazine

"Jacquelyn Small is a living exemplar of what she teaches.
Her life and this book sets before us the precise steps we can
take to realize our divine potential. I recommend it with all
my heart."

> —BARBARA MARX HUBBARD, co-founder,
> Foundation for Conscious Evolution,
> author of *The Revelation*